A Special Kind of Parenting

Meeting the Needs of Handicapped Children

Book Review

Good, Julia Darnell and Reis, Joyce Good.
A SPECIAL KIND OF PARENTING.
LLLI, 1985.

> Handicapped children have special needs which challenge their parents' emotional and physical resources. This book can guide parents through the problems and help them discover their disabled child as an individual. The authors cover both facts and feelings about handicaps, parents' reactions to the initial diagnosis, the grieving process, and effects on the marriage and the rest of the family. They also provide suggestions for choosing the programs and professionals best suited to a child's unique needs and abilities. (See NEW BEGINNINGS Mar-Apr 1986.)

Available from LLLC, No. 280

Book Review

A Special Kind of Parenting

Meeting the Needs of Handicapped Children

Julia Darnell Good
and
Joyce Good Reis

La Leche League International
Franklin Park, Illinois

© 1985 Julia Darnell Good and Joyce Good Reis
All Rights Reserved
Published by
  La Leche League International, Inc.
  9616 Minneapolis Avenue
  P.O. Box 1209
  Franklin Park, Il 60131-8209
First Printing July 1985
Printed in the United States of America
Cover Design by Wolferman and Stuffelbeam
Library of Congress Catalog Card Number 85-080903
ISBN 0-912500-27-1

I wish to dedicate this book to my husband of thirty-seven years, Dr. Jim Good, who always encouraged me to stretch my wings and fly.

Julia Darnell Good

Contents

	Foreword	ix
	Introduction	xiii
Chapter 1	**A Special Child Is Born**	1
	Feelings of Loss • The Need to Be Together • Benefits of Breastfeeding • Providing Breast Milk Despite Separation.	
Chapter 2	**When Awareness Is Gradual**	13
	Delayed Diagnosis Is Common • Emotions Play a Part • When to Seek Help • Choosing a Physician • The Team Approach • Parents' Rights • Making Decisions.	
Chapter 3	**Grief, Coping, and Acceptance**	29
	Parents Experience Grief • The Stages of Grief • Other Emotions • Adjustment Does Come.	
Chapter 4	**Strengthening Your Marriage**	45
	Difference in Reactions • Importance of Communicating • Spending Time Together • Outside Interests.	
Chapter 5	**Special Nurturing**	55
	Belonging to a Family • Learning to Make Decisions • The Need for Discipline • Dealing with Sibling Rivalry • Less Than Perfect.	

Chapter 6 **Learning at Home: The Preschool Years** **69**
Infant Stimulation Programs • Readiness for Preschool • Learning at Home • Learning Can Be Fun • The Younger Child • Enjoy the Outdoors • Music and Make-Believe • Patience Is Vital • Learning by Doing • Social Skills.

Chapter 7 **The School-Aged Child** **83**
Goals and Expectations • Learning and Growing • Educational Opportunities • Learn the Terminology • Residential Schools.

Chapter 8 **The Teen Years** **97**
Decision-Making Skills • Communication Skills • Social Life and Sexuality • Spending Skills • Achieving Independence.

Chapter 9 **Handling Medical Emergencies** **109**
Airway Management • Control of Bleeding • Cardiac Resuscitation • Fractures • Convulsions • Fever • Choking • Poisoning • First-Aid Supplies • Permission for Emergency Care.

Chapter 10 **When a Child Is Hospitalized** **121**
Approaches Can Vary • Intensive Care • Is Weaning Necessary? • Prepare the Child • The Child's Fears • How Parents Can Help • Expect Some Reactions.

Chapter 11 **Communicating with Medical Professionals** **139**
Learn Their Language • Finding a Doctor • Discussing the Problem • Parental Decisions • Hospital Personnel.

Chapter 12 **Helping the Family Under Stress** **149**
How to Offer Help • Support Groups.

Chapter 13 **Those Who Care** **155**

Chapter 14 **One Family's Experience** **165**

Bibliography **169**

Foreword

    This book is a reflection of an idea whose time has come. It is a "how-to" book written with wisdom in an easygoing, pleasant fashion. It is a personal document and therein lies its beauty.

    Life is a challenge, and life with a handicapped child is even more of a challenge. Wisely, the definition of "handicapped" is questioned by the authors. This book, warmly written, will enable a parent to more easily cope with a problem, and help parents learn to share their problems or tragedy and grow stronger, rather than having their relationship disintegrate.

    This book will be helpful not only to parents but to physicians and other professionals who are involved in the care of special children. It will show the professionals how their own sense of inadequacy may reflect upon their handling of the parents in the situations described. I hope it will influence how much they will allow parents to interact with the handicapped infant.

    If it does nothing else, this book will help relieve parents of much of their guilt regarding their handicapped child. It is shown, and oft repeated, that breastfeeding and the closeness it occasions, helps parents to love and accept their handicapped infant more. A special acceptance of one's special baby is seen at La Leche League meetings.

There are some great descriptions in this book. Grief is described as both the sense of acute loss and the realization of unmet expectations, of what might have been. Grieving is a living experience, an opportunity to come away from pain with growth. Chapter 3 on "Grief, Coping, and Acceptance" is one which should be read, re-read, and referred to again and again. This volume will help the parents of a child with a handicap share each other's strengths and face the future together, stronger, rather than have this handicap act as a wedge driving them apart—to divorce. By helping the parents cope, this book will ultimately help the parents to help the child cope.

It is essential for both parents (and grandparents and involved relatives, too) to read this book. It will help them to understand what each is experiencing as well as what their child is experiencing. Many practical suggestions, almost all dealing with increased communication, such as setting aside daily time to talk to your spouse, are given by the authors.

I'm delighted to see that learning in a warm and loving home is stressed in the preschool years, rather than in school. This is in concord with my own observations in a thirty year pediatric practice. The authors state: "Because a child learns best when he feels secure, wanted, and loved, parents are usually the best teachers."

The authors, in effect, do for parents, what the government has done for children in the 1975 Education for All Handicapped Children Act with the Individualized Education Plan.

A helpful definition is given—that the handicapped child is not usually a sick child, but a well child with a disability. As a practicing pediatrician, I have seen numerous children who are having all sorts of problems, both at school and home, until a learning disability was diagnosed and therapy begun. Trusting your instinct as parents is valuable advice. Thoughtful suggestions on where to seek help in evaluation and diagnosis are presented.

This book helps to establish communication, the all important factor in child rearing, or in life itself for that matter. Parents should be given alternatives. Decision-making is their right and their responsibility ultimately.

Chapter 9 on handling medical emergencies should be required reading for all parents and the reader will find most useful the complete listing of organizations which can provide information or aid in Chapter 13.

The greatest tribute to this book will come, not from me, but from scores of parents, who, having read it, will say: "Oh, if only there was such a book as this when our handicapped child was born!"

I only wish to add that this book includes such wisdom regarding child-rearing that it will prove of great benefit even to parents of a child who has no "handicap." The authors state: "The most valuable gift a parent can give his child is a positive self-image." This book helps parents do just that.

This book deals with honesty and is written honestly. The poignant stories shared by other parents add to the validity of this work.

The ingredients of knowledge, common sense, and compassion mixed in the proper proportions by the authors, have resulted in a book which should prove helpful to parents of children with a disability, but on a more broad scale, to all parents. The thesis, "If you are not your child's advocate, then who will be?" is clearly and articulately presented.

Arnold L. Tanis MD, FAAP

Introduction

A Special Kind of Parenting is born of one author's experience as the mother of two handicapped children, Joseph, who died at the age of three months, and David, who was born nine years later and is now a teenager. She recalls:

> When David was five years old, he attended the Crippled Children's Center Preschool. When I walked with him to his classroom at the beginning of the school year, I couldn't look at the other children because of the tears in my eyes. I hurried down the hall, looking neither right nor left, trying not to see the four- and five-year-old children on crutches and in heavy leg braces. I surreptitiously wiped away my tears, hoping no one would see me crying in the hall.
> After a few weeks, I began to notice the sounds of the children laughing and playing. They sounded just like any other children. I risked a peek at what they were doing and noticed a particularly cute child. I soon learned his name and talked to him. Then I began to talk with the other children as well. As I began to know them as individuals, I was able

to relax and enjoy them with no more tears. How could I cry for them when they were happy children, laughing and playing? Then the truth hit me, these children weren't handicapped, I was! It was true that they couldn't run or do many things that other children can do, but that didn't prevent them from enjoying life. They learned what many five- and six-year-old children learn. They didn't dwell on what they could not do, but enjoyed what they could do.

Learning to know the children as people, as individuals, was the key to overcoming my fears. Squeamishness and pity were replaced by admiration for the courage and persistence of the children working hard to perform many activities most of us take for granted.

This is a story shared by many parents, of times of overwhelming sadness and great joy, of hopeless despair and courageous triumph. As one mother explains, "I guess it all boils down to children—all people start as children who need love and approval to grow. There doesn't have to be a distinction made as to what kind of children. They're all marvelous."

In our society, handicapped persons are frequently referred to as "special" in an attempt to remove the stigma attached to the word "handicapped." We believe that every child is a special child, having unique and individual needs. We also recognize that there are many types of handicaps—conditions that interfere with life functions. Among them are the attitudinal barriers that society or the individual imposes on life. During an interview of a group of handicapped adults, one young man responded that he wanted people to see him, not as handicapped, but as a person who happened to be in a wheelchair.

This book is intended for parents who view each of their children as an individual, regardless of his or her special needs. In parenting we try to meet those needs, to provide our children with nurturing love which will enable them to grow into independent, self-sufficient adults. Although the child may have special needs related to his condition, he also has the same needs and feelings that every child experiences. As one father reminds us: "Life has so much to offer even to the handicapped child. The beautiful seasons, birds flying, flowers growing, sweet scents, bright sunshine, gentle winds, and most importantly, a loving, warm, accepting relationship with another human being."

It is important to acknowledge that when a handicapped child is born, there is an immediate and serious impact on the parents and the whole family unit. Guilt, fear, blame, and chronic stress frequently take their toll on the marital relationship. Divorce rates are much higher among parents of handicapped children than for society at large. Part of this book will deal with the emotional needs of parents, with strengthening their relationship, and developing a support system. As parents reach out, first to the medical community and later to family and friends, they hope to find compassion, understanding, and empathy, yet so few persons know how to react and respond in positive, loving ways. We offer suggestions to those who assume helping roles.

It is not our intention to provide answers to "why?" but we can offer suggestions for "how": how to cope with unmet expectations, how to develop a strategy for daily living, how to meet emergency situations, how to allow love to grow, how to work with medical professionals as a team, how to engineer your environment for maximum growth and development, how to meet the needs of parents and siblings, and how to parent the handicapped child.

Louise Wills, a dear friend and the mother of a handicapped child, offers this definition: "A handicap is something that makes success harder, not impossible. We are all handicapped in some way; it is really a matter of degree." Indeed, we would have been very handicapped in writing this book if it had not been for the contributions, assistance, and patience of many people. We owe much to Louise and Charles Wills, to Doris Valenti, Cathy Angell, Kathy Baker, Jacie Coryell, Janice Pickett, and the other parents who shared their experiences and ideas with us, to James Good and Anne Cave for their fine editorial eyes, to David, for permission to expose so much of his life, and to all our children. They have taught us much about acceptance and love, and have given us opportunities to grow.   *J.D.G. and J.G.R., 1984*

"What is real?" asked the rabbit one day...

Real isn't how you are made...
It's a thing that happens to you...
When a child loves you for a long, long time...
Generally, by the time you are Real...
most of your hair has been loved off and your eyes drop out...
But these things don't matter at all,
because once you are Real you can't be ugly,
except to people who don't understand."

MARGERY WILLIAMS, *THE VELVETEEN RABBIT*

Chapter 1

A Special Child Is Born

"We're not sure what it is, but something is wrong with your baby."

To all appearances, the baby seemed normal but an alert nursing staff had observed that he had not urinated in the twenty-four hours since birth. During an examination, the pediatrician found an enlarged kidney. He presented the news to the father and together they approached the mother. The doctor realized that the parents' reaction often depends on the manner in which emotionally shocking news is related. Therefore, he preferred to discuss such news with both parents at the same time so that they might be mutually supportive.

Although the physician did not have a diagnosis at this time and could not answer many questions, he tried to be reassuring. He went on to explain that more tests would be performed, necessitating transfer of the baby to nearby Children's Hospital. Arrangements were made for the newborn's father to accompany him in the ambulance and he was even able to baptize his child, a ritual which gave comfort to both parents.

Because he was able to be with his child and participate to some degree in his care, the father was able to postpone some of the emotional impact. However, the mother, alone in her hospital room, felt overwhelming shock, disbelief, isolation, and anxiety. She wondered if she might have done something during the pregnancy to cause the birth defect. Even when her husband was with her, and they were experiencing similar feelings, they found that grief can isolate one spouse from the other. The mother recalls, "I was determined that our tragedy would strengthen our marriage rather than divide us. We turned to each other for comfort and strength. We learned to share our sorrow and disappointment."

The mother's sympathetic obstetrician discharged her from the hospital earlier than usual so that she would not have to be with other mothers and their healthy babies. Meanwhile, the baby was undergoing emergency surgery to provide drainage from his kidney after tests had shown the ureter was not connected to the bladder. Both parents were able to be with their baby very soon after his surgery. They were encouraged to visit him and participate in his care even in the intensive care nursery. This helped them come to grips with reality and to become acquainted with their child. Their immediate shock was replaced with curiosity about their infant's condition and prognosis. By discussing their fears and questions with the nurses and physicians, they were better able to understand the baby's problems and make informed decisions about his care and treatment.

Feelings of Loss

Whenever the news comes that the baby has a birth defect or a medical problem of some kind, it is a great shock to the parents. No one expects a tragedy to happen. Intense feelings of loss occur when the outcome of the birth is less than positive and not what the parents imagined. The parents' first reaction is often, "Why us?" It is not uncommon for a mother to experience a sense of abandonment when separated from her baby, especially when the separation is both physical and emotional. She may feel guilt about some event during pregnancy which she focuses on as contributing to the defect. Each parent may blame the other in spite of reassurance that neither was at fault.

Many times couples do not experience the ideal treatment which this family had: Husband and wife were together when the news of the birth defect was presented and the father was encouraged to be with the baby during the transfer and permitted to perform a comforting religious act. Their physician recognized their needs and the needs of the baby. Often it is not the news itself which is most difficult to assimilate but the manner in which it is shared. In a questionnaire used by the authors, many parents expressed anger over the way they were told of their child's disability. Frequently, they were not together and thus were not able to support each other. Or the information was inadvertently revealed by someone other than the doctor. Occasionally, the information was inaccurate because the physician did not have a complete diagnosis or prognosis.

In the case of a Down Syndrome baby, parents are frequently advised to institutionalize the baby or even to allow him or her to die, although there is no way to determine the severity of retardation or prognosis at birth. The physician operates from his experience and knowledge which may be limited in some circumstances.

The nursing staff often unintentionally ignores the mother of a handicapped newborn. The nurses may be busy with other mothers and babies and believe that the mother without her baby does not need nursing care. Because maternity nurses do not deal routinely with loss and grief, they may feel a sense of inadequacy when the birth of a handicapped child occurs. A nurse's ability to cope with emotional trauma depends largely on her personal experiences with death, and like many people, she may feel uncomfortable and unable to offer support to the parents.

The Need to Be Together

The parents' emotional reaction does not depend solely on communications with the physician nor on the support of the nursing staff. The parents' own attitudes and experiences play a role in how they react to the birth of a handicapped child. The emotional impact is greatly influenced by the manner in which they are allowed to interact with their baby. Contact with the newborn may depend on the infant's condition. Since many handicaps involve several body systems, or the extent of the medical problems may not be fully recognized at birth, the baby may require constant observation in a special nursery. Some babies who are premature or who have respiratory difficulties may be placed in incubators in an intensive care nursery. In any event, the parents and baby need to be together as much as the baby's condition permits.

Most physicians and hospitals recognize this need and allow parents access even in intensive care nurseries. Parents are encouraged to participate in their infant's care while he is in an incubator. Studies have shown that the more contact the parent has, and the more responsibility for the baby's care, the greater his or her self-confidence will be in his or her parenting ability. In most hospitals today, parents are permitted to don sterile gowns and reach through the openings of the incubator to touch and stroke their baby. Even when the monitoring equipment, intravenous lines, and catheter restrict taking the baby from the incubator, the parent can stroke a cheek, hold a tiny hand, and talk to the infant.

Previously, physicians believed that limiting parents' access to the baby would prevent or ease some pain should the baby die. Many parents, however, have found that being with their infant and caring for him actually helps them because it enables them to deal with the reality of the situation. Contact relieves so many fears and doubts about their ability to love and care for the baby. It gives parents some tangible activity through which they can demonstrate their love and it provides them with the reassurance that they have done what they could and spent whatever time they had with the baby, should he die. Becoming acquainted with their baby allows parents to focus on what *is*, instead of what might have been. Some fears are alleviated as parents find facing problems directly holds less threat than what they had been imagining.

Drs. Marshall Klaus and John Kennel, formerly of Case Western Reserve University School of Medicine, conducted studies of mother-infant behavior after birth and popularized the concept of "bonding," which involves the growth of love and attachment between the parents and baby. Bonding, they found, can occur at any time and is facilitated by the opportunity to participate in the infant's care. Time together is the only requirement for bonding to occur. Bonding is doubly important when there is a medical problem. It helps alleviate many of the anxieties, such as, "Will I be able to love my baby? Is he attractive? Can I care for my baby? How will we manage?" So many questions become less significant, fears less threatening, when the parents can touch and hold the baby.

Janice Pickett, the mother of a baby who required surgery immediately after birth, explains, "Being able to be with my baby was all that mattered to me. Until he was able to nurse, I spent two to three hours with him, three or four times a day. I would just sit and touch him on his foot, or leg, or arm, any place he did not have a tube. Spending time holding and nursing my baby was essential for my well-being as well as his."

Another mother, Louise Wills, speaks of her husband's needs. "Those were the worst days—he at home with three preschoolers, me in the hospital with only the nursing periods for comfort. I really think rooming-in would have been a boon. There was no way except through the glass case for Charles to see Erika. How could he know that she was a real baby, not a nightmare, when he wasn't allowed to see or touch or hear her?"

Studies have shown there are fewer pathological grief reactions among mothers who have been allowed to touch their babies. Bonding can occur even though the baby may be in an incubator in an intensive care nursery. Attachment between parent and child is promoted by physical contact, touching, stroking, singing, talking, holding the baby as much as possible, and breastfeeding.

Benefits of Breastfeeding

In the past ten years, physicians have begun to recognize the importance of bonding; now, many are also acknowledging the role breastfeeding plays *especially* when there are problems with the baby. Breast milk contains immunoglobulins which protect the baby against diseases. This is especially important to the infant whose body systems may be immature or overwhelmed by a disability. Breast milk has lysozyme, an enzyme also found in tears, which destroys the protective coating of many bacteria cells so that the living white cells within the milk can attack the germs. Interferon is another constituent of breast milk that fights against virus, and breast milk also provides lactoferrin and transferrin that prevent the growth of harmful bacteria in the intestinal tract. The bifidus factor in mother's milk allows beneficial bacteria to flourish in the intestines.

Breastfed infants have fewer allergies and illnesses, especially respiratory infections, diarrhea, and eczema. Studies show that the incidence of illness and infection in breastfed babies is one-third that of formula-fed babies. Breast milk contains all the nutrients, in the exact proportion, that an infant needs. No formula can be as complete. For example, breast milk contains taurine, an essential amino acid which contributes to optimal brain growth. Each mother's milk is specifically suited to her own baby; the breast milk of the mother of a premature baby differs from that of the mother of a full-term baby, to meet the special needs of the preterm baby.

Gail Reid, whose baby was premature, explains, "Saving my milk and taking it to the hospital were, for us, tangible efforts to be parents to this tiny human being. Having the best nutrition possible was her birth right and I wanted to provide it for her."

Breastfeeding provides many benefits to the mother as well. It encourages the uterus to return to its pre-pregnant state. The contractions that occur during breastfeeding help to prevent postpartum hemorrhage. The hormones secreted in response to stimulation of the nipple also promote a sense of calm and peace. *Breastfeeding can be a normal experience in emotionally trying situations where little else seems normal.* Louise Wills, the mother of a Down Syndrome baby, remembers:

> The morning after Erika's birth, I was anxiously awaiting nursing time when the pediatrician came in and told me the baby was in an incubator. What fears ran through my mind! "She has Down Syndrome," he said.
> The nurses were very kind. They brought Erika to me and undressed her so I could see she was all there. They left her with me to nurse, and that's when I discovered how comforting breastfeeding is for the mother. No matter what, I could do something good now. And, although the suck was not quite as strong, and the rooting not as sure, still it was there. And while we were nursing all seemed well.

A distinction must be made between the total act of breastfeeding and the supplying of breast milk. While the milk is, in itself, valuable to the baby, the breastfeeding relationship involves much more. Breastfeeding has many advantages for both the baby and the mother.

Charles Wills, Louise's husband and a psychologist, expresses a father's feelings about breastfeeding. "It seems more precious when an infant is mentally

Jordan Blaugrund at age four weeks enjoys a few quiet moments at his mother's breast on the day before his heart surgery.

handicapped. From the very moment that child is born he will need tremendous quantities of love and acceptance. That close relationship at his mother's breast goes a long way toward fulfilling those needs. This is not to say that a bottle-fed baby cannot receive love and acceptance. But breastfeeding is so much more intimate, so much more meaningful to the mentally handicapped. The relationship is established early and lasts many months—months when a handicapped child is most vulnerable both physically and emotionally."

Breastfeeding contributes to a woman's feelings of motherliness and self-confidence. The mothers who founded La Leche League write in THE WOMANLY

ART OF BREASTFEEDING, "The breastfeeding relationship itself makes us more sensitive to all his [the baby's] needs, so we are quicker and surer in devising ways of meeting them."

The skin-to-skin contact during breastfeeding is important to both mother and baby. It is a valuable part of the bonding process. Because a baby who is in an incubator can suffer from sensory deprivation, breastfeeding is especially important. Touch improves the baby's respirations, as Dr. Ashley Montagu writes. "The cutaneous stimulations the baby receives from the mother's caressing, from contact with her body, its warmth and especially the stimulations about the face, lips, nose, tongue, and mouth received during suckling are important in improving the respiratory functions and through this means, the oxygenation of the blood."

Sucking is another important need common to every baby. One mother was told her baby was too retarded to learn to suck. The mother, however, persisted. She relates, "If Sara had been born normal and healthy, she would have been breastfed, so why give her formula because she happened to be labeled 'retarded' and had to be fed, for a time, by a tube? Because of her suffering, she deserved even more the closeness of a nursing relationship." Sara and her mother eventually established a long-term breastfeeding relationship which her mother believes made up for their time of separation.

Providing Breast Milk Despite Separation

Even when mother and baby are separated or the infant is unable to nurse, the mother can still provide breast milk for him. Most hospitals have electric pumps which the mother may rent or she may purchase or rent one for home use from a distributor. Some mothers find hand pumps or hand expression are also effective. It is very important that a mother be encouraged to breastfeed or to pump her milk for the baby because of the many advantages to both, especially because breastfeeding allows the mother to contribute to the baby's well-being in a unique and satisfying way. Karen Schaeffer-Murphy's daughter was born with a rare form of cancer, necessitating two month's hospitalization for treatment. During that time, Karen pumped her milk. She describes her feelings. "I am so thankful for both of us that I held onto the hope that someday I'd be able to nurse my Regan. Nursing seems to give Regan as much pleasure as it does me. She makes up for lost time, meeting her sucking needs as well as her need for breast milk."

Breastfeeding bridges the separation, providing an emotional link between mother and baby akin to that which was present before birth and lessening the impact of their separation. Another mother summarized her feelings about how breastfeeding helped her through the difficult times:

> When Chad was a few weeks old, he was hospitalized for intestinal surgery. I continued to pump my breasts and hoped for the day when we would be reunited. At long last Chad and I were together again, and within three days he was totally breastfeeding. As I look back at Chad's first year, I'm sure that breastfeeding and the closeness that comes with it helped me to love and accept him just as he is. There were still lots of tears, sometimes falling on my special baby as we rocked along, so alone, yet so close. I had many anxieties about the future.

Even if you have not been able to breastfeed or express your milk in the hospital—perhaps you did not have the information or support necessary—you can initiate nursing when the baby comes home from the hospital. You may use a pump to help develop and maintain the milk supply, or you may try to relactate at a later time. Assistance with either procedure is available from La Leche League International. Informational pamphlets are available on these topics and a wide variety of other special situations, such as Down Syndrome and premature birth. La Leche League also provides mother-to-mother support and help that is so important to mothers facing difficulties. One mother commented that she found a special kind of acceptance as well as information at La Leche League meetings. For help in unusual circumstances or information about the closest La Leche League Group, contact La Leche League International. (See Chapter 13.)

References
Countryman, Frank. Grieving is a living experience, *LLL News* 23(Sept-Oct):96, 1981.

Craver, Diane. Nursing our special baby, *LLL News* 22(Nov-Dec):81, 1980.

Good, Judy. Breastfeeding the baby with Down Syndrome. La Leche League International publication No. 23. Franklin Park, IL, 1985.

Reid, Gail. A dream that came true. *LLL News* 18(July-Aug):57, 1976.

Schaeffer-Murphy, Karen. Regan's story—born with cancer. *LLL News* 22(Sept-Oct):81, 1980.

Womanly Art of Breastfeeding, The. La Leche League International, Franklin Park, IL, 1981.

Chapter 2

When Awareness Is Gradual

When David was born he was in a breech position, bottom first with both legs up. His legs were badly bowed for months afterward, but this is not unusual for a breech baby.

When his legs did not straighten by six months of age, his father, a physician, x-rayed David's legs. He found that in addition to the bowing, the long bones were not of the proper density. Consultations with a pediatrician and a radiologist followed, and it was found that all his bones were similarly affected.

Osteogenesis imperfecta, "brittle bone disease," was considered as a possibility, although blood tests did not support this diagnosis. Of course, his parents were alarmed. His mother recalls, "We hoped that somehow it was all a mistake and that he was all right even if his bones appeared to be fragile."

Although a little small for his age, David developed normally, crawling at six months and walking at a year of age. Outwardly everything seemed perfectly normal until shortly before his second birthday. He was playing with a brother when there was a snap, followed by a scream of pain. He had fractured his femur (thigh bone). He spent the next three months in a full body cast.

Two weeks after the cast was removed, he tried to stand and the tibia (shinbone) broke. One fracture followed another and it was soon realized that, although lab tests didn't confirm the diagnosis, clinical evidence established that David had *osteogenesis imperfecta*.

When David was seven and in the hospital with another fractured femur, he suffered a grand mal seizure. He was placed on a precautionary dosage of phenobarbital. At age eleven, he began having more seizures and epilepsy was diagnosed. His mother explains, "I was most dismayed by this development because of his bone problem. Sometimes just the muscles pulling on his bones as he has a seizure has caused fractures. Somehow it seemed unfair . . . he had more than enough problems!"

David's mother continues, "Even after the bone condition had been diagnosed and throughout several years of repeated fractures, our full realization of David's problems and the extent of his handicap was gradual. Later, even though he was having seizures, I didn't accept that he had epilepsy. Acceptance of the epilepsy also came to me gradually."

David's story is typical of a child whose congenital handicap was not discovered until some time after birth. The parents suspected something was wrong, they experienced ambivalent feelings—"Yes, there is something; no, there isn't," and "He is small for his age, but he is developing normally." In this situation, a crisis led them to the clear-cut knowledge that there was definitely a disability.

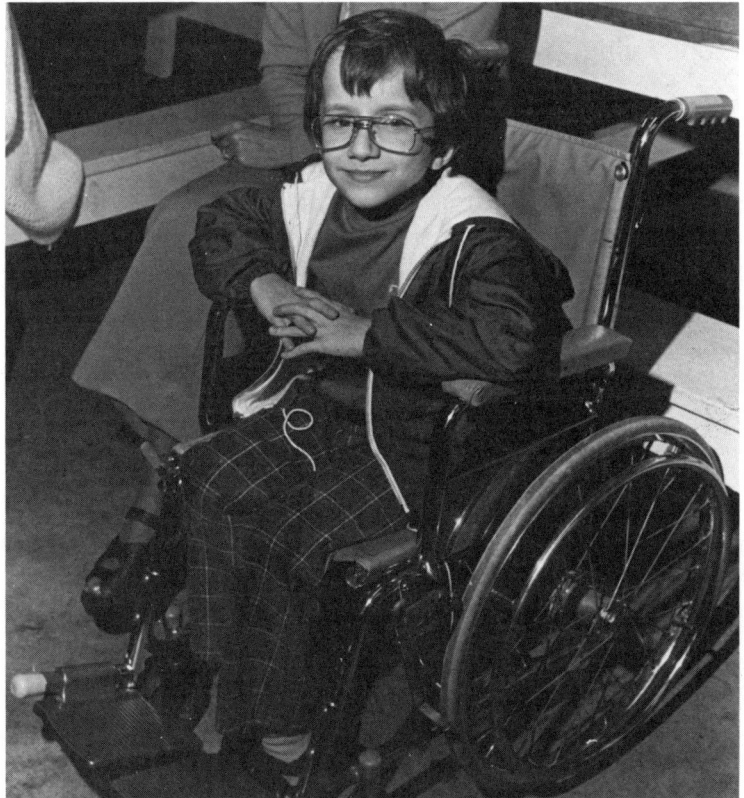

David Good, six years old, gets around in a wheel chair.

David's experience is also typical of many handicapped children in that he has multiple problems. *Osteogenesis imperfecta* affects his bones and teeth and has resulted in smaller than normal size. In addition, he has developed epilepsy.

Delayed Diagnosis Is Common

According to a report by the Surgeon General of the U.S. Department of Health and Human Services, two percent of liveborn infants have handicaps that are discernible at birth. By age five, ten percent of children are considered handicapped. More handicaps are found in the first five years of life than those which are readily diagnosed at birth.

For the parents whose child has a disability that is not diagnosed at birth, the experience of confirming the handicap can be a long and painful one. "Confirming" rather than "discovering" is usually the case, because most of the time, the parents suspect there is a problem and must convince their physician to look for the cause. For some families, this requires a long search and many trips to many physicians.

The parents themselves are often handicapped, first of all, by the normal emotions which involve denial ("He'll grow out of it") then by bargaining ("If we attend church every Sunday, he'll be better"), and finally by their lack of influence with medical professionals. Some mothers have been accused of being overprotective and neurotic rather than observant and justifiably concerned. Physicians often find it difficult to trust in parental instinct and judgment and to acknowledge that parents can be the experts in the knowledge of their child and his development.

A mother shares her anguish by saying, "Our daughter is developmentally handicapped. . . . The doctors blamed her lack of development and growth on her cleft palate for a year, while all my research told me that this was not a cause."

One study at the California School for the Deaf found that fifty percent of the parents were told by physicians that nothing was wrong with their child and not to worry. Physicians are not the only ones who can misdiagnose a disability. Another mother relates, "When the test results were in, she [the school psychologist] said that since he is a bright child he was compensating so well that they couldn't detect it from casual observation. I refreshed her memory to the fact that I had been telling them of the problem for some two-to-three years."

It must be said, too, that the nature of the handicap may make diagnosis more difficult. Only twenty percent of disabled persons between infancy and twenty-one years of age have sensory or motor impairment. The remaining eighty percent have some degree of mental retardation, ranging from learning disability or language dysfunction to severe retardation. Some such limitations may not be recognized for years. The confirmation of one of the milder handicaps may be complicated because symptoms may point to several disabilities. For example, the child who is a slow learner, inattentive, and disruptive may have emotional problems, a learning disability, a hearing loss, or minimal brain dysfunction. Cathy Angell, a mother, adds, "Children with emotional problems are handicapped, but you can't tell just by looking at them. Often their problem is thought to be misbehavior and lack of discipline."

Lack of responsiveness by medical and other professionals adds to the emotional impact of the situation. Cathy Angell continues, "People sympathize with the blind child, but not with the antisocial or unmanageable." Another mother says, "It is a very frustrating feeling knowing that your child is emotionally hurting and being unable to get others in responsible positions to believe you. I have tried to use the school system and have found personnel to be either noncooperative or blatantly ignorant of the emotional needs of LD (learning disabled) students and their families."

When one mother finally convinced school authorities to listen to her concerns, she found that "the school psychologist did not apologize for not believing me previously. She simply blamed her mistake on my son's intelligence. She offered no information about LD children other than to talk about his IEP (individualized education plan) meeting and the educational implications of his possible use of a tutor."

The recognition of a problem may come gradually to the parents. Doris Valenti tells us that when their physician suspected their son might have Down Syndrome, she and her husband searched their memories, trying to compare this baby to his older siblings. While waiting for test results, they experienced swinging emotions, "Yes, he is; no, he isn't."

Emotions Play a Part

Mixed and painful emotions may force the parents to continue looking for answers, with the hope that someone will disprove their suspicions. But for many parents, there is a certain amount of relief when the diagnosis is confirmed. One mother explains, "Although we had a whole new set of concerns to handle, it was a comfort knowing what the 'something' was. It had a name and there was a way to treat it. No longer were our problems merely suspicions." Knowledge replaces ignorance and gives the parent greater ability to deal with the situation, thereby increasing self-confidence.

Whether the diagnosis of a handicap comes at birth or several years later, the parents face the same emotional crisis and passage through the stages of grief. When the diagnosis comes after months or years of searching for answers, the parents may feel additional guilt for not having found help or recognized symptoms earlier. They may also have greater anger and resentment toward a medical community who may not have been able to make a rapid or accurate diagnosis.

The parents of an emotionally handicapped child experience an even greater burden. A mother shares her feelings. "Emotional problems in young children are so difficult. Books suggest that if you follow your child's lead and meet his needs he'll be healthy and independent. I know I've made mistakes—what parent doesn't—but I question whether they were enough to harm Brian in this way." In another context, a mother suffered the anguish of being accused of child abuse when her daughter was bruised during a grand mal seizure.

When the diagnosis comes after a period of months or years, the parents may have less fear of the future because they have lived with their child and they know they can handle many daily situations. The revelation may have less impact on their lives. They do not face the added pressure of integrating a new baby into the family, which is, in itself, stress-producing. However, any time it is discovered that a child has a handicap, parents and family will be under stress. This is a time of increased vulnerability, a time when the most difficult decisions must be made and choices seem to be so final and exclusive.

Of those contributing to this book, parent after parent suggests that the most important step for the mother and father of a handicapped child is finding another person in whom to confide, someone who will listen and understand. One mother, Jacie Coryell, explains, "I think parents need to have someone to share with, someone who doesn't criticize, someone who will help with the child and respect him or her no matter what." Doris Valenti adds, "The support of family and friends is very important. You may worry about what to say or not say to the parent following the birth of a handicapped child, but sharing genuine feelings, maybe saying, 'I don't know what to say, but my heart is with you,' helps most."

When to Seek Help

When should parents suspect there is a problem and how should they proceed? It is important to remember that the handicapped child is not usually a sick child, but a well child with a disability. There are, of course, some children with chronic illnesses or repeated infections which are later diagnosed as due to some medical condition, but for the most part, the handicapped child is a well child.

A general rule of thumb is: If the child lags six months or more behind other children of the same age, he should be evaluated. Any child experiencing difficulty in any particular area should also be examined for some underlying problem. Trust your instinct as parents—most parents do recognize that something is amiss long before there is a clinical diagnosis.

If you suspect something is not quite right, approach the physician with facts, not feelings alone. You will need some concrete reasons for your suspicions, such as, "Children of this age should be sitting up, reaching for toys, following objects with their eyes, and my child is not doing these things," or "my other children walked by twelve months and this child is eighteen months and showing no signs of being ready to walk."

Try first to eliminate other possible causes on your own. Educate yourself about child development. Investigate other possibilities; for example, hidden allergies are responsible for many symptoms from bedwetting to behavioral problems. Then get the best medical advice, but retain your own judgment—you are the expert about your child.

Choosing a Physician

You will want a doctor who is medically competent and who is open to new ideas, willing to talk with you and explain all the options, and ready to listen empathetically and to respect your feelings and parenting goals. If you live in a small community or rural area, you may have to travel to a nearby metropolitan area to find such a person, but it is well worth it. Remember that you are paying for his or her services and you have the right to discharge the doctor and seek another.

You might begin looking by asking friends or a parent group for recommendations. Your family physician or pediatrician can also suggest a specialist with whom he has had experience. Make an appointment for a consultation during which you can explain the kind of care you expect and the qualities you require in a physician. If one parent cannot be present for the visit, the other can include him or her verbally by saying, for example, "My husband and I believe . . ." Such honest, up-front communication will help to establish rapport and understanding.

The physician should be willing to take the time to explain the child's problems in a language that you and the child, if he is old enough, can understand. Communication is a two-way street and you will also want a doctor who will take the time to listen to you and respect your values.

You will want a physician who understands and enjoys children. Look about the office. Is it a cheery, pleasant place to visit? Is it child-oriented? How does the physician's staff relate to children and parents?

Be sure to inquire about after-hours availability. Will he come to the home to see the child, if necessary? How can you reach him after office hours? Does he share coverage with another doctor? What hospital does he use? What pharmacy does he recommend?

You may need to search to find the right doctor for your family, but the efforts are well worth the time and energy because it is important that you understand and trust each other in order to work together for your child.

Most pediatricians are trained to recognize symptoms of illness, but spend little time learning to evaluate behavioral and developmental problems. If your physician cannot find the problem, seek a second medical opinion. Rather than accepting the opinion of one person, request a team evaluation.

One author recommends that parents seek help at the best-known teaching hospital in their area. Ask for the pediatrics department and find out whether they offer services for developmental evaluation of young children. Check on the procedure, waiting time, costs, etc. Other alternatives for help are a parent group, school psychologist, local mental health center, community diagnostic and treatment center, or social service agency.

When the problem is not an obvious one, the team approach is especially useful. The disciplines involved might include neurology, psychology, language development, and audiometric evaluation. The extent of involvement and degree of handicap, the effect of the disability on the child's mental, physical, emotional, and social life, the child's general medical and psychological health may be assessed in reaching the diagnosis. Again, the single most important person is the involved and informed parent who can provide detailed observations, family history, prenatal and birth history.

In her book, *Ever Since Adam and Eve,* Terry

Hekker writes, "When you don't trust your instinct, it's easy to be taken in by experts and authorities. But the truth is, very few people are as smart as you believe they are, including yourself, and you are probably smarter than you think you are. It's a mistake to put such faith in experts that you don't question, especially when dealing with doctors, teachers . . . child psychologists. They may be proficient, but nobody knows your child better than you do."

The Team Approach

The goals of the team approach to assessing the child should include:

- The establishment of mutual trust, clear and open communications, honesty, consistency, and a non-threatening environment.
- The incorporation of the family into a plan of action. Long-term and short-term care goals should involve parental needs as well as the child's. Decision-making must be rational rather than emotional, and the parents need accurate information and empathetic support from the team.
- Maintaining the parents as effective, confident caregivers and advocates of the child.

Parents' Rights

As parents, you have certain rights when dealing with the medical profession. You should be completely informed about your child's diagnosis and prognosis. Although the information may be limited, especially when the diagnosis has been a difficult one, such as minimal brain damage or emotional disturbance, the physician should be frank and honest with you. You need as complete a picture as possible in order to make informed decisions about your child's care and treatment.

Parents have a right to be supported emotionally. It is normal to feel guilt and to blame yourself. You need reassurance that most of the time there is no definable cause for the disability. Even when blame can be fixed, such as when a child is injured in an accident which may have been the parent's fault, the medical professional should remain non-judgmental. The cause of the handicap is irrelevant. Parents can only deal with the present and need help to overcome natural feelings of guilt and the tendency to place blame in order to become productive members of the caring team. If institutionalization is an alternative that you must consider, you should be reassured that such a decision does not mean you are abandoning your child.

If you are unable to work positively with your physician, you have not only the right but a responsibility as well to discharge him and seek another with whom you will be more compatible. As a matter of courtesy, you should explain to the physician why you are discharging him. If the reasons are listed clearly and unemotionally, the physician may learn something from this experience which will help him in future dealings with patients.

Parents have the right to be fully informed about proposed medical procedures. You should receive complete explanations of all tests and treatments. It is the obligation of the medical professional to inform you about the necessity, purpose, and goal of tests or treatments, and to seek your parental consent.

In addition to rights, parents have certain responsibilities. Your role in your child's treatment is that of advocate. You should ask questions and when your queries are exhausted you can summarize with, "Is there anything I should know that I have not asked about?"

Parents have a decision-making role which requires not only being informed, but also accepting responsibility for decisions. You are the ones who will live with your child, support him, and educate him. In sharing with your physician, you must neither withhold information nor avoid following directions. If certain things do not seem right to you, discuss them with your doctor.

Keeping medical records is another parental responsibility. You should know the medications your child receives, the treatments, vaccinations, illnesses, allergies, etc., he has had. In addition to being informed about your child's handicap, you should be prepared to handle any routine care and in addition, any foreseeable emergency situation. In discussing your child's prognosis and future, you can ask the physician what complications or medical emergencies you might expect and how to deal with them.

Making Decisions

Whether the realization of the child's handicap comes immediately after birth, following an accident, or more slowly and gradually, parents share common experiences. There is the passage through the stages of grief, and the establishment of a relationship with a physician or other professionals. Along the way, the parents learn what their rights and responsibilities are as parents.

While experiences may be similar, solutions differ for each family. Many decisions can be postponed and solutions worked out over a period of time. Many parents, when faced with a decision of whether or not to institutionalize their child, opt to try keeping him in their home to evaluate their ability to care for him while continuing to meet the needs of other family members. Such decisions are not irreversible, and as one mother points out, "Not making a decision to institutionalize and seeing how it goes at home, *is* making a decision."

There have been many changes in the way in which disabilities are viewed by our society. Louise Wills compares today with the time when her daughter was born with Down Syndrome. "Twelve years has made some difference in the way professionals view handicaps; certainly there appear to be more support groups and books. Back then, when I said, 'Yes, she will nurse, and run, and speak, and read,' many professionals were patronizing and even gently suggested an institution—if not at once, then certainly as she grew older. But time and perseverance and the ability to let go, to let Erika try her wings, have paid off."

New sources of information or help may be forthcoming, sometimes unexpectedly so. As David's mother explains: "My husband and I were leaving a meeting one evening, when a friend inquired about David's health. A doctor overheard our conversation and volunteered that he was a pediatric orthopedic specialist interested in *osteogenesis imperfecta*. We discussed it with him and eventually transferred David's care to him. He believed in the use of high doses of vitamin C and in brief casting. This treatment was often very painful for David and we had to take extra care to prevent re-fracturing, but the innovative technique worked. David improved dramatically. He went from four fractures a year to about one.

"While we still have times when we ask, 'Why me? Why my child?', there are just as many times when we are optimistic. Medical science just might come up with answers and new methods of treatment."

References

Benderly, Beryl Lieff. *Dancing Without Music.* New York: Anchor Press, Doubleday, 1980.

Hekker, Terry. *Ever Since Adam and Eve.* New York: William Morrow, 1979.

Report of the Surgeon General's Workshop on Children with Handicaps and their Families. U.S. Department of Health and Human Services, 1982.

Strauss, Susan. *Is it Well with the Child?* New York: Doubleday, 1975.

Chapter 3

Grief, Coping, and Acceptance

"Each of us experiences the same emotions but in different ways," explains Doris Valenti, the mother of a son with congenital heart defects and a son with Down Syndrome.

No matter when the parents learn of their child's handicap—whether at the time of birth or later in life—they begin to grieve immediately. Grief is both the sense of acute loss and the realization of unmet expectations, of what might have been. Doris continues, "The child you expected is not the child you have." Another mother, Jacie Coryell, adds, "When you are expecting a baby, you don't plan on having a handicapped child. All I want is [for] life to be normal, with no stares, no looks, no uneasiness. I don't want to be different." Jo Harmon-Blaugrund explains, "Let's face it, we all think that by doing the 'right' things we are guaranteed perfect children. Life's not like that."

While the feeling of acute loss diminishes with time, the feeling of a continuing loss remains. Jacie continues, "I'd drive down the road and see girls Amy's age with skates over their shoulders and start to cry because she will never go off to the rink with friends." Another mother comments, "I wonder sometimes when the crying will stop. But it never does. The crying will never stop."

Charles Wills adds, "It is difficult to put into words one's feelings and thoughts on being informed that a handicapped child has been born into your family. The shock and numbness wear on for many days and even months. Actually, those feelings can remain for life."

Parents Experience Grief

Grief is not always a negative emotion. It can serve as a catalyst for interpersonal growth and can be harnessed to provide the momentum to seek answers. Grieving is a living experience, an opportunity to come away from pain with growth. Any life situation which involves great emotional shock can evoke the psychological response mechanism known as grieving. Elisabeth Kubler-Ross, MD, in her work with the dying and their families identified five stages of grieving:

1. Denial
2. Anger
3. Bargaining
4. Depression
5. Acceptance

The body uses these stages to adapt to psychological stress. Passage through the stages is an ongoing process, especially when the parent is dealing with the handicapped child. When death occurs, the grieving has some resolution and the passage through the stages seems to have a more definitive course. With the hand-

Jonathan Valenti celebrates his first birthday.

icapped child, grieving is ongoing, with passage through each stage coming over and over again.

More than one stage may be experienced at one time. Progress from one stage to another may not necessarily indicate some psychological growth or adaptation. As one mother discloses "Even now, I still get down about many things. I find myself going through the stages over and over again."

Emotional response differs with each member in the family unit. Each passes through the stages at different rates and times, which can make supporting and nurturing each other more difficult. How an individual handles this type of stress depends on his previous experiences, attitudes, and emotional and physical strengths. Doris Valenti describes herself as a "survivor," believing that her attitude enables her to be more accepting of the crises in her life. For another mother, peace of mind is less easily found and her anguish is apparent in a quote from a letter, "What a terrible person I am to have this much resentment of an innocent child. Why haven't I been able to work this out? What will it take?"

Shock, a physical body mechanism which conserves energy, precedes the stages of grief and protects the individual from dealing with emotional trauma until he is able to proceed into the stages of grieving. Then, too, many parents find their memories of the grieving process dim as the body attempts to shield itself from emotional trauma.

These intense emotions and shock can erase moments of joy and excitement following the birth. Doris Valenti describes the first few weeks after the birth of their Down Syndrome baby: "We were confused and hurt! How could this happen to us? We pushed aside those beautiful moments of Jonathan's birth and replaced them with many days of questioning, pain, and tears. Adjustments were many. The first month of Jonathan's life was a blur of much crying, bitterness, self-pity, and worry about the future."

The Stages of Grief

Denial is the first stage. This is a temporary response which prevents emotional overload. It involves screening out psychological pain. The parent may ignore information or facts, project anger onto another person, especially a physician or nurse, or rationalize. For example, one mother, unable to accept her son's illness, attributed his withdrawal and listlessness to shyness. In this stage, the person may avoid talking about what is happening, he may escape into work, watching television, overeating, sleeping, taking drugs, or drinking an excessive amount of alcohol.

Many times, in order to spare the parents, a physician will recommend institutionalization of their child, and this may be a form of denial. Some parents keep that image of the perfect child in their minds and spend unrealistic amounts of time and money seeking cures.

Denial involves anxiety and fear. While fear can arise because of both actual and potential problems, parents of a handicapped child usually experience fear that is grounded in reality. Because it is not a neurotic fear, it may be more difficult to deal with and may be overwhelming. Neurotic fears respond to conventional therapy; fears based on reality do not. But, fear can be controlled. When the parents realize that they can direct those same energies toward learning about their child's condition and prognosis, they are no longer allowing the unknown to immobilize them. What has already occurred cannot be prevented, but many times, parents find that problems which exist in reality are less threatening than those which they had imagined. Fear serves the useful purpose of directing the search for knowledge.

Denial can be a long-term emotion. Jo Harmon-Blaugrund's son Jordan was born with a heart defect which will require many operations. She describes her husband's reactions as they faced another surgery: "My husband seemed to be very rational through this whole two years with Jordan, but I have always felt he found it difficult to face the problem except when absolutely necessary. Recently he told me that he won't be able to block out the impending open heart surgery. He has been able to block it out up to this point, but he knows he can't continue to do so just because he's afraid of what might happen."

Anger can be healthy or destructive depending on how it is expressed. It is okay and even healthy to feel anger. Repression or denial, though, can lead to physical and emotional illness. Expressing and resolving angry feelings is a healthy response to emotional pain, helping the person to fight fear. Some anger is reasonable, however, anger rarely exists alone. It is often combined with hurt, fear, disappointment, misery, desperation, frustration, and rage. As one mother comments: "I resent [my child] for what her handicaps have done to me . . . I resent people staring at her . . . I hate the thought of her future . . . ."

Another explains, "As long as I thought I could make her okay, I tried, but when I was told that she wouldn't ever be normal, it was over for me. I started for the first time to really resent her . . . . I began to wish she'd just die."

In an article in *The Exceptional Parent*, one woman wrote of wishing for her son's death, of feeling embarrassed when he acted "retarded," bored by his repetitious conversation, and enraged when he exploited her impatience. In subsequent letters to the magazine, other parents shared their similar feelings and told how this woman's admissions helped to console them.

Such anger is a normal part of the grieving process, and is one that continues throughout life. At milestones when the child might have experienced some achievement and did not, or when faced with the comparison to another child, perhaps a peer, the parent may experience the same intense anger as during the initial passage through the stages of grieving. A parent elaborates, "It was just devastating. You suddenly find out that your child is not going to be normal. Your child is not going to grow up to be president.... When you see a normal child going down the street, you want to turn away. You don't want to look. And for a while I hated everything. I hated my son, I hated me, I ignored my husband, I was jealous of my daughter because she was normal."

Anger is often accompanied by self-pity, and many parents share what one mother expresses, "I think I feel more sorry for myself than for my daughter." Doris Valenti adds, "I thought I had paid my dues with Matthew who was born with a congenital heart defect. When we were told that Jonathan had Down Syndrome, we felt much bitterness and self-pity."

It is okay and even healthy to experience anger. Learning to handle it, to channel it into constructive energy is part of accepting and learning to cope with the situation. Jacie Coryell offers, "I think you need to be able to go into another room and cry, throw pillows, break glasses, something to get it out so it doesn't come back on the child."

Six simple steps can be used to learn to express anger constructively:

- Be aware of your emotions. Is the anger masking some other emotion?
- Admit your feelings, even if only to yourself.
- Own your feelings; they are yours and it is okay to feel as you do. Accept responsibility for them.
- Investigate your feelings. Are they based on reality? Is there some aspect of the situation which might be changed that would lessen anger.
- Match what you are experiencing to what you are saying. A discrepancy between what a person is saying and feeling brings confusion to relationships with others and results in a breakdown of communications.
- Integrate your personality by using your emotions, intellect, and will to grow as a person. You can choose to focus on anger, bitterness, and frustration or

you can try to put these negative emotions aside and get on with life.

Bargaining occurs when the parent implores God, "If I do . . . my child will be whole." This is an irrational step sometimes taken by grief-stricken parents until they are able to face the reality of the situation.

Depression is anger turned inward, producing guilt and recriminations. Professional help is needed if depression includes suicidal thoughts, major changes in sleeping or eating patterns, or if it continues for a long period. Some find taking additional B vitamins to be helpful in combating the symptoms of depression. Depression can also be a healthy stage when it allows the time for marshalling inner strengths and establishing healthful habits which are stress-reducing.

Other Emotions

In addition to experiencing the five stages of grief and their attendant emotions, parents also feel many other emotions. Louise Wills explains, "All who have birthed such a child know the hurt, the guilt, the fear, the pity of others, the surprise with which the decision to breastfeed is greeted, the wonder at the fact that you are not leaving this child behind."

Parents commonly experience a sense of isolation. This is not unusual for new parents in general as they try to meet their child's needs. But for the parents of the handicapped child, the isolation is much greater. It may be due to the physical limitations the child's disability imposes, or it may be a response to the lack of understanding the parents perceive from family and friends. Doris Valenti comments that the amount of information about Down Syndrome now available has increased acceptance of her son, but it is still difficult for her grandparents who relate to a time when the handicapped child was spurned by society.

The parents of a handicapped child are more vulnerable to meddling from outsiders—from medical professionals, relatives, and friends. After a few painful contacts, they withdraw and avoid situations which might cause further pain. This only serves to increase the parents' sense of isolation.

One mother points out another feeling, "Pregnancy and birth are such miracles, they make one feel so much like God. It's difficult sometimes to face the stark reality of one's humanness, to realize that out of such a god-like state can come something less than perfect. It's kind of a lesson in humility."

Guilt is another feeling frequently and acutely experienced by the parents of the handicapped child. All parents occasionally have ambivalent feelings about and toward their children or their parenting skills. But generally, temporary irritations and anger are handled well enough. Parents of the handicapped child, however, are more apt to set impossible expectations for themselves as parents. They may believe that they should never become angry or scold the child. When they feel resentment about the time and energy the child requires, they impose feelings of guilt on themselves. The parent berates himself or herself for the normal feelings of anger and resentment. He is often unable to communicate these feelings to his spouse, which creates a wall of silence where there might have been shared feelings, mutual compassion, and support.

Guilt can drive a parent to do too much for the child, or guilt may produce the opposite effect. It can lead the parent to ignore the handicap. In either event, guilt serves as a wedge between the parents, and the persons who are best able to support each other are driven apart.

To all parents, a child symbolizes the future and our contribution to society. Our sons and daughters embody unspoken but profound hopes. We enjoy a certain self-satisfaction in seeing them accomplish goals and grow toward independence. The parents of a handicapped child may find their own sense of adequacy threatened by the handicap. It may be difficult to remember that love and satisfaction can be derived from any child who is reaching his potential, regardless of what that potential is. As Louise Wills comments, "The dictionary defines a handicap as 'a disadvantage or encumbrance which makes success more difficult.' Not impossible, just more difficult. It's a broad enough definition that each of us fits into it at one time or another."

Acceptance occurs when the parent can acknowledge that there is a reason for this child's existence, although that reason may never be understood. Acceptance involves "letting go" of grief, a *conscious, daily action* which enables the individual to focus on what is, instead of what might have been. Through acceptance, the answer to "why" becomes irrelevant.

Acceptance involves acknowledging that you have problems, and you and your child may face an uncertain future, but, as Doris Valenti believes, "Things will work out—maybe not the way you had planned, but in that is the growing."

Acceptance does not ameliorate grief; acceptance controls it. It involves giving yourself permission to grieve, but realizing that you are the master of your emotions and need not allow grief to control you.

Learning to live from day to day is part of acceptance. Many parents find that when they are able to "live for today," they can deal better with their anger, bitterness, and frustration. This does not mean that they never feel negative emotions again. For most, grief is a lifelong process, and so too is the task of dealing with it. As Jo Harmon-Blaugrund admits, "I still find myself asking why my baby was born with a defect."

Acceptance on the parents' part is important in helping the child accept himself. The biggest problem of a handicapped child is often not the disability, but a low self-image. Children mirror the image their parents convey to them and their self-concepts are learned through their relationships with others, most importantly their parents.

Charles Wills points out: "Society has engendered in all of us the feeling that we must not deviate from the norm, that if we do, we are unusual and are to be pitied. We have been taught to be productive, contributing members of society.

"A Down Syndrome child cannot be this way. And yet is his or her life any less precious because he lacks these features?"

The future of a handicapped child often seems bleak. But as one mother reminds us, "No one knows what the future holds." In an interview with parents of handicapped children, the parents were asked to complete this sentence: "I hope my child . . ." One-third used "happy" or "happiness" in their responses, another one-third included "fulfilled," "contented," or "well-adjusted." Only two mentioned "success."

Acceptance and coping go hand-in-hand. Coping involves accepting problems, considering alternatives, making decisions, and following through with plans. No matter what special needs the child has, setting goals is helpful. If the parents can form a plan which is flexible enough to meet the child's and their own needs, this can put problems into perspective and bring equilibrium to the situation.

Not only must the parents develop their own coping mechanisms, but often they must help other family members as well. Jo Harmon-Blaugrund explains that her grandmother was very close to the family, but she could not accept Jo's son's heart problems and surgery. Jo continues, "Until recently she always said, 'You shouldn't even think about him going back into the hospital. He might never have to.' She denied that he has some serious defects which must be corrected surgically." Finally, after listening to her grandmother patiently for some time, Jo noticed a change. Her grandmother said, "I guess you shouldn't think that, should you? You're going to have to handle it when it's time."

Acceptance involves developing a daily coping plan:

- ***Acknowledge your right to grieve*** and give permission to other family members to grieve. Recognize that all emotions, whether negative or positive, are a part of life's experiences, but that you can control their influence and be responsible for your feelings.
- During the grieving process, it is normal to have difficulty concentrating on tasks, even those of daily living. ***Break each task down into simple steps***, perhaps even listing these and crossing each off as it is accomplished. Simplify your life and the demands on your time and energy wherever possible.
- ***Train yourself to look for something positive*** in all experiences. You can learn to think more positively by choosing what you pay attention to and what you say about it to yourself and others. Give yourself time to develop a habit of focusing on positives. Part of self-discipline is restraining impulses

to pity yourself or your child. When negative thoughts creep in, do something mentally demanding and positive.

• ***Every person has at least one asset,*** perhaps an engaging smile, a special sense of humor, attractive eyes, or childish innocence. Concentrate on that quality which you most admire or like in your child. You define yourself and others by what you say, so refer to these appealing characteristics in conversations with others.

• ***Meeting your child's needs fosters a sense of caring*** which grows into love. Recognize that you are indispensable to your child. Because of your relationship, you are the expert at ascertaining and meeting his needs, and no one can usurp that role.

• Because grieving involves physiological as well as emotional responses, **the body needs special care during this time of stress.** Every parent needs adequate rest, exercise, and a nutritious diet. It is easy to neglect a proper diet when you are emotionally overwhelmed, yet this is a time when you need an especially healthful diet. Vitamin C and the B vitamins are depleted by stress and your doctor might recommend supplements.

In addition to physical needs, you have emotional needs as well. Keep your self-esteem high by seeking support from others. Don't be afraid to ask for help or encouragement when you need it.

• ***Learn to manage stress productively*** by developing a daily stress-reduction program. Stress can be debilitating if allowed to accumulate. Schedule time for yourself to pray or meditate. Include exercise, preferably in the fresh air, as often as possible. Exercise releases endorphins, a body chemical which increases a feeling of well-being.

• ***Replace negatives in your life with positives.*** Take a look at your environment first. Do you like the colors in your home? Are the rooms bright and cheery? Would some changes give you a lift? Positive thoughts beget a positive outlook. Write out your favorite quotations and hang them where you will see them frequently.

Put a small mirror in each room and remind yourself to smile every time you pass it. Each small step will add up and improve your outlook.

• **Share with others.** There is a maxim which says, "Friendship divides grief and doubles joy." Develop a support system and learn to share with friends both the sorrows and the happiness. Grief has a tendency to isolate people. Take deliberate steps to open communications with others. Tell the person that you aren't seeking answers or solutions, just someone who will listen and accept.

The support of others who care, or perhaps those who have been through similar experiences, is very important. Doris Valenti found that meeting other parents of Down Syndrome children was very helpful. "They were happy, coping people," she explains, "living their lives with handicapped children, some of whom were more severely affected than my own son."

Janice Pickett also found support in talking with a mother whose child had a similar condition. She recalls, "She talked to me about her son and his surgery. She gave me one piece of advice for which I will always be grateful because it made a difference in how I saw my child and how others saw him . . . . A simple idea but a concrete one that helped my perception of my child."

While some parents benefit from associating with parents who are in similar situations, others find the support they need in a group they are already associated with. Louise Wills attended one meeting of a just-forming parents' group, but found her La Leche League Group was, "Enough for me!" Doris Valenti seconds this, "The caring and acceptance from La Leche League mothers outweighed the trauma of seeing normal babies at the meetings."

• **Think small.** When the business of living becomes overwhelming, look at the everyday details you may be missing. Watch the sun rise, seek the first flower of spring, catch a single snowflake, examine a

Jonathan Valenti sits propped in a basket to play with his older brothers Peter and Matt.

spider web, listen to your child's breathing, smell the vanilla in the kitchen cupboard, tickle a kitten's ear, collect a bouquet of dandelions, make a wish on an evening star, blow bubbles with dish detergent, take a bubble bath. Look for beauty, design, and simplicity in your environment.

Adjustment Does Come

Many parents take comfort in the fact that, as they adjust to their child's handicap, they find it is not as devastating as they originally believed it would be. They still have times of fear, doubt, anger, depression, and frustration; every parent does. However, they choose not to waste precious time on negative feelings. They involve themselves in the business of living each day as it comes and developing daily coping plans. Doris Valenti describes what helped them in the first weeks. "As we grew in our acceptance of our son's specialness, we realized that, after all, he was a baby whose basic needs were the same as any other child. Again, we remembered the joyful night of his birth and realized that our family had been given a gift! Our lovely birth experience, the joy we all shared, the first days of celebration had created a firm bond that could not be broken. What a great beginning for this sweet little boy!"

References

Featherstone, Helen. *A Difference in the Family.* New York: Basic Books, 1980.

Harmon-Blaugrund, Jo. Jordan's Story. *Ohio South Outreach, LLL News* 25(Mar-Apr), 1983.

Kubler-Ross, Elisabeth. *On Death and Dying.* New York: MacMillan, 1969.

Linn, Dennis and Linn, Matthew. *Healing Life's Hurts.* New York: Paulist Press, 1978.

Chapter 4

Strengthening Your Marriage

"What makes a marriage work? Drawing together and supporting each other," say Mick and Beth Ball, whose oldest son was born with a malformed leg and hand and learning disabilities.

A handicapped child's problems can constrict a couple's life at every point. The usual problems which exist in most marriages are amplified in force and intensity under the additional strain of parenting the handicapped child. Emotional distancing, exhaustion, fear, anxiety, guilt, resentment, and financial concerns strain the marital relationship. Fatigue and cumulative stress often interfere with communications between husband and wife, and this breakdown is the greatest threat to any marriage.

"We long for normalcy," continues Mick Ball. "We've had one problem after another. Handicapped children have all the usual problems plus those caused by their disability. As the problems mount up, you often wonder 'When will I have time to get on top of all this?' "

All too often the stresses lead to marital disruption and divorce. "Divorce rates are as much as 50% higher in these families than in those with healthy children," writes Michael Rothenberg, MD, head of the Pediatric Liaison Division at the Children's Orthopedic Hospital and Medical Center in Seattle. The chronic drain on physical and emotional energies takes its toll on the marital relationship.

A child's handicap can affect the marriage in four ways: It initiates powerful emotions in the parents; it influences the organization of the family and its relationship to society; it may become a symbol of shared failure and a focus of intense guilt; and it provides fertile ground for conflict.

The grieving period can begin the estrangement unless the parents take steps to avoid it. One mother recalls, "I was determined that the tragedy of our son's death would strengthen our marriage rather than divide us. We turned to each other for comfort and shared our sorrow and disappointment." Several years later, this same family had a second child with handicaps and the parents found their grieving different. "In the case of a handicapped child, the grief goes on, over and over. Even when we had come to grips with the problems, there was fresh grief whenever something else came up or when we just saw another child run and play, knowing that our son will never be able to do that. Because of our previous experience with grief, we were able to turn to each other for support."

Difference in Reactions

People react differently to grief and experience the stages of grief at different rates. Some want to talk about every detail, requiring great patience of the listener. Others internalize their emotions and prefer not to discuss them. For one couple, it was the wife who was eager to have the problems diagnosed, almost glad to have them out in the open, for then she could grieve and get it over with. The husband, however, was devastated by each new problem and angry with his wife for accepting them.

Doris Valenti recalls that her husband's reaction to grief also differed from her own. "He internalizes feelings. But because we have shared our experiences, his awareness has increased and we are both better able to deal with our emotions now."

Expressing your feelings to another person can be very difficult for many people. Traditionally, men have been taught to internalize emotions, especially those which deal with nurturing behavior. However, women are equally repressed by social stigmas attached to experiencing feelings, especially those of anger.

Mick Ball explains that he had carved out a role as protector of his wife and family and felt that he had to be the strong spouse who couldn't show feelings. He learned, "You can't control your feelings but you can decide what you are going to do with them."

The Balls believe that the key is to work on sharing emotions and needs. They are involved in Marriage Encounter, which helps couples to learn to express their feelings. They recommend this or any other form of counseling for a couple experiencing difficulties communicating. Even a healthy relationship can benefit from talking with a trained helper.

Another parent elaborates on the importance of dealing with feelings. "When you recognize that each spouse reacts differently, it is easier to discuss feelings and share the load. When suffering or pain comes there are two ways to react. You can put the blame on your spouse and be angry or you can realize that this is going to solve nothing and only hurt your partner. Feelings can act as a wedge between you or they can draw you closer to each other and strengthen your marriage."

Importance of Communicating

You can begin sharing feelings by giving each other permission to grieve and hurt, to express anger, disappointment, guilt, resentment, and fear. Realize also that establishing a daily coping plan will enable you to move forward with life. Grieving will be a lifelong experience, and it is necessary to come to grips with its powerful and negative emotions in order to live a productive life.

The marital relationship in itself is no guarantee that feelings will be shared. A couple may need to work to develop a safe environment for each to express their feelings to the other. Couples tend not to share feelings because they get into a rut, they are busy with other activities, perhaps they don't want to "rock the boat," or one or the other may be out of touch with inner feelings.

Communicating feelings first requires trust and acceptance that feelings are neither right nor wrong. Secondly, a couple needs time. Try to set aside ten to fifteen minutes daily for talking with your spouse. This may not be easy when your child's handicap already places many demands on your time and attention, or when there is separation because of hospitalization. But setting aside time to talk daily can soon become a habit. It then requires less foresight and planning.

If you are unaccustomed to sharing feelings verbally, you might begin by writing your spouse a letter. Be open and honest about how you feel and about your relationship. Concentrate on reaching out to the person you married and let it be known that you accept his or her feelings. Ask your spouse to tell you what he or she is experiencing, to describe feelings as fully as possible. Put aside decision-making and problem-solving for that brief time. Exchange letters with your spouse and read them carefully. They are the basis for dialogue.

Touch while listening. Hold hands, or touch your spouse's shoulder. Make contact, "touch" with the eyes as well. Focus on rekindling the feelings of togetherness you experienced during courtship. Use "I" messages—"I feel . . ." and "I need . . ."—rather than "you should . . ." statements.

Listen attentively to your spouse. You may tend to think through your next statement while the other is still speaking and miss much of the content and meaning of what is said. Suspend that inner voice. If you are unsure that you understand what your spouse is saying, repeat his or her words and ask for clarification. Try to be sensitive to the unspoken messages as well.

Financial concerns are often a tremendous problem for the parents of a handicapped child. The Balls' son had eight operations and although many expenses were covered by insurance, there were many others which were not. Beth explains, "One of the biggest problems is that you feel out of control. You don't know where to look for help." They eventually found that the Shriners would help cover the cost of their son's prosthetic leg which must be replaced as he grows.

It is often essential that one parent be at home to care for the child. Originally husband and wife may have planned for both to be employed. Thus the family must adjust to living on one income. When much of the burden of caring for the child falls on one parent, resentment can set in. For example, in the case of a child with arthritis, the mother spent a great deal of time manipulating painful joints and dealing with an angry and uncomfortable child. When the father came home, he was perceived by the child as the parent who rescued him from the pain associated with his mother's care.

The father who is not as involved in his child's care often feels less adequate to provide for his child's physical needs. He may also resent the demand the child imposes on the mother's time and energy.

Spending Time Together

Couples need to spend time together, but when children are young or problems add to the normal pressures, finding time together can be very difficult. It need not be a large chunk of time, nor time which is devoted exclusively to the two of you. Many couples build times of togetherness into their daily routines, sharing household duties or cooking. One mother explains, "Ours is a family kitchen. My husband is at the stove, I make a salad, a baby is on the floor pulling pans from the cupboard, a toddler sits on the counter sampling carrot slices from the salad, and an older child is setting the table. We may be crowded but we're together, having a good time."

Another mother says that Saturday mornings were their times together. The children were permitted to "camp" on the living room floor and watch cartoons. When they were younger, their mother provided a cooler stocked with fresh fruit and granola for a fast and easy breakfast that the children could manage on their own. Even the toddler who slept with his parents would join the Saturday morning television viewing for a short time, leaving the couple a few minutes alone.

Some couples shower together, conserving water as well as time. One mother points out an additional bonus, "As our children are growing older they like to eavesdrop on our conversations; the shower gives us privacy and drowns out our voices."

One wife suggests reserving fifteen minutes at bedtime to talk to each other; another sets her alarm clock ten minutes early every morning for a leisurely few minutes with her husband. The father of a handicapped child realized that he and his wife needed more exercise as well as more time together. His solution was to buy a bicycle for two. Other couples walk, skate, or work in the garden together.

When the children are young, a walk or a drive in the car provides diversion for them and an opportunity for you to talk. One mother confides, "As our children grew, we went from whispered tones in the front seat, to spelling certain words, to spelling them backwards." Another activity which may fit into your lifestyle is family camping. Tents and sleeping bags can be adapted to fit many of the special needs of handicapped children. The flexible and relaxed environment of a family outing can bring a welcome break in routine. One mother sums it up, "I think many marriages just die from boredom. You become so caught up in everyday tasks that you forget to have fun."

Finding time together can be especially difficult when the handicapped child needs constant care. In some communities, respite care in which trained persons provide nursing care, is available for short periods.

Another mother found that non-professionals could often meet this need. "Our family and friends were wonderful. They gathered around us and I have never felt such a loving aura of support." Some parents make arrangements with other families to trade off caring for each other's children for brief times. In this way the parents of the handicapped child can get away yet be reassured that a responsible adult is caring for the child. This deep friendship with other parents helps to alleviate the feelings of isolation faced by the parents of a handicapped child.

The same stresses which interfere with communications also affect the sexual relationship. Fear of pregnancy or of having another child with a handicap may add to the parents' anxiety. They worry about their ability to have a normal child, yet they may feel guilty when another baby is born. The parents may wonder if enjoying the normal baby means that, in some way, they are rejecting the handicapped one.

Genetic counseling may answer some of the fears parents have about their ability to have a normal child. For many couples there are no definite answers, and they may benefit most from the informal counseling available from a parent support group.

Outside Interests

Marriage is a growing, ever-changing relationship. It is nurtured by communicating one's deepest feelings in an atmosphere of trust, respect, and concern. As you grow, it is important for you and your spouse to grow together. Even when the responsibilities seem overwhelming, working together, sharing feelings, and supporting each other enable a couple to cope with the most formidable problems. As Mick Ball puts it, "We support each other even though we sometimes feel as if we are fighting the world." As the couple become mutually supportive, they insulate themselves from stress and build a stronger foundation for the future. One mother summarizes, "Every time you face a problem and handle it together, you grow stronger and more able to cope with the next one."

Many couples find that when time and energy permit, involvement in some activity or organization beyond the family draws them together. For some families, becoming active in a church gives them the satisfaction of working within a community as well as providing the support of friends who share their concerns. Marriage Encounter gave Mick and Beth Ball an opportunity to help other couples through their own experiences.

Repetition and boredom can be a problem for the home-bound parent of a handicapped child. Involvement in an activity or organization outside the home can meet the need for self-actualization and fulfillment. Such activities may involve the parent and child together, such as with Scouts, family vacations, church, or social activities.

Even a brief amount of time spent on new projects on a regular basis refreshes and recharges coping batteries. The parent who is able to develop some personal interests or devote time to a project outside the family can add spark to the marital relationship.

Many mothers find that being active in La Leche League meets their needs for involvement with others. Few organizations in our society emphasize the importance of the family and the nurturant role of the mother as well as La Leche League does.

Strengthening the marital relationship involves both activities which draw the couple together and ones which encourage personal growth in the family members. As one mother recommends, "Never lose sight of having fun as a couple and as a family."

References

Havron, Dean. Sex and depression: coping with the
    chronically ill child. *Sexual Medicine Today*, Nov:14, 1981.

Chapter 5

Special Nurturing

"The important factor in parenting is that the parents are comfortable meeting their child's needs," Kathy Baker, mother of a blind child, tells us. "People say to me 'I wouldn't let *my* child push me around like that!' But they are on the outside looking in, and they don't understand what the feelings are of parents who are tuned into their child. We are performing labors of love, not making martyrs of ourselves."

Selma Fraiberg, professor of child psychoanalysis at the University of Michigan School of Medicine, explains, "Need and the satisfaction of need are indispensable components of all primary human bonds." By meeting your child's needs consistently and noncritically, you provide an atmosphere for maximum growth and development.

In addition to meeting your handicapped child's greater physical needs, you must deal with his emotional and psychological needs. These include his need to feel connected, "bonded," to the significant people in his life, to know he can trust his developing values, goals, and self-direction, to learn how to use his own resources, to appreciate his uniqueness, and to experience self-respect.

The way you feel about your child's disability is the chief factor determining his attitude toward it. Your child reflects your feelings and attitudes. Therefore, it is tremendously important that you learn to control anguish, anger, depression, and anxiety and convey a sense of hope, caring, and as much as possible, normalcy. This will help your child develop positive feelings about himself. Self-image encourages the child to live up to or down to the image that others, especially his parents, have of him.

The greatest problem of the handicapped child is often not the disability itself but a poor self-image. Surveys have shown that many persons with severe physical disabilities don't generally regard themselves as handicapped, while others with relatively minor limitations think of themselves as severely handicapped. A person's view of his handicap may be more disabling than the physical problem itself.

Self-image is important because the extent of the handicap depends partially on attitude. Those who cannot accept their limitations and learn to focus on what they *can* do, instead of what they cannot, will never feel a sense of satisfaction from what they do achieve.

Self-esteem has been defined as the satisfaction with oneself that one feels when needs are met, either by one's own capabilities and resources or through interaction within the environment. Self-esteem determines how the individual acts, learns, relates, feels, and works; it is expressed in actions and it promotes behavior which reinforces itself.

Special Nurturing   57

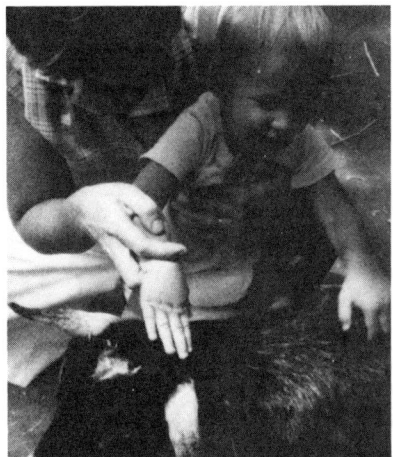 

Kathy Baker provides a variety of experiences for Nicholas.

Positive self-esteem is necessary to respond to self and others in positive, growing ways. People who have positive self-esteem feel good, look good, are effective and productive, and care about themselves and others.

You can meet your child's self-esteem needs by treating him with a casual, natural attitude. Initially, your child may view a handicap as a punishment for being "bad." Reassure him that this is not so. Explain his handicap to him in ways he can understand.

Never say anything to others when the child is present that you haven't said or wouldn't say to the child. Encourage your physician and other medical professionals to adopt these same guidelines.

Along with your trust, a child needs to be treated with respect. A child who is treated with respect develops respect for self and others. Give your child as much privacy as you would anyone else. This is especially important during hospitalization or medical treatments in the home. As his advocate, you can safeguard his privacy.

Approach him at his level. If he is in a wheel chair, bend down so you can easily establish eye contact. Whenever possible, treat your child as you would any child his age. There will be times when he will regress or he may always be less mature, so be prepared to be flexible and adjust expectations accordingly. By encouraging him to reach for his goals, you will help him as well as reinforce your belief in his ability to meet reasonable expectations.

Be open and honest with him about his limitations. Encourage him to develop a realistic view of his handicap. This does not mean limiting his options nor withholding optimism. Rather, expect him to meet reasonable standards of behavior and performance. Do not permit behavior you would not accept in your other children just because he is handicapped. (Obviously, this does not apply to behavior over which the child has no control, such as spastic movement which may accompany cerebral palsy.) Find ways that he can contribute to the family, perhaps through the performance of simple chores.

Belonging to a Family

Every child needs to know how he fits into the family and society. Your guidance and expectations of certain behavior will help your handicapped child feel this sense of belonging to your family. Teach him how to relate to others. He will need to know how to cope with others' reactions to his disability, how to handle pity, and how to put others at ease. One mother commented that her son's sense of humor was an invaluable aid in helping others to relate to him and forget his handicap.

Over and over, let your child know how much he means to you. Acknowledge those positive character-

David Good helps with the dishes.

istics which make your child different. You can do this automatically in daily interaction. Touching and holding, establishing eye contact, listening and talking, sharing feelings and activities convey the message that you enjoy being with your child. Look for occasions to tell him that you feel good about him. "I used to think that the way to teach my children to do things better was to explain to them what was unacceptable when they did something wrong so that they could correct their actions the next time," admits one mother. "Then I learned how discouraging this was. Now, I use positive reinforcement and my children literally blossom when they are told what a good job they are doing."

Praise your child, being careful that the praise is genuine and specific. It is better to compliment a specific action rather than offer general and vague statements, such as "You're a good boy." Praise him whenever possible for his skills at relating to others, for example, "I'm proud of the way you shared your game," or "You're doing very well learning to handle anger." Some children are uncomfortable when praised by their parents and another approach might be useful. A mother explains, "Even though our son had problems with a low self-image, he rejected my positive comments and praise. But he did enjoy hearing good things about himself from his grandmother. Whenever he had some special achievement, I would suggest he tell her about it or I would call and relate it so that she could offer the praise he needed to hear."

Parents can provide all the positive, affirming messages and yet the child may still have a negative self-image. Each person is responsible for determining his own self-esteem. One mother tells us this story:

> When our son was in first grade, he was a miserably unhappy child and we had a real battle getting him going in the mornings. We used a simple story to teach him about his responsibility for his own self-esteem. "You can be like the hippopotamus who lives by the stream and spends all his time wallowing in the mud. Or you can be a bird who flies over all the mud and soars into the sky. It is up to you which you will choose to be."
>
> He still chose to wallow in self-pity for a few more weeks, but he knew we weren't going to take responsibility for his feelings. We continued to provide as much reinforcement and affirmation as we could, and slowly it began to work. Our six-year-old hippo became an eight-year-old bird.

Learning to Make Decisions

Encourage your child to develop decision-making skills. In the young child this might involve making simple choices between two toys, two shirts, or two snacks. As the child matures, you can offer more alternatives and soon he will be generating his own alternatives. Decision-making allows him to experience a sense of power, which is necessary as he learns how to use his own skills and resources to affect his environment. Avoid "should" and "should not" statements. Instead, tell him how his actions affect you. For example, replace "You should not leave your books on the table," with "When you leave your books on the table, it makes extra work for me," or "You should do your homework early because we are having guests," with "We're having guests tonight, and I want you to meet them, so you will have to decide when to get your homework done."

Every child seeks approval from his parents. It is an ongoing active process which tells the child he is valued. When a child knows he will receive approval without having to seek it, excessive demands for attention diminish. The more secure the child feels about himself, and the more independent he is encouraged to be in his home, the more confident he will be in exploring the world around him.

This combination of security and independence is especially important for the handicapped child. His disability often requires greater attention from his parents, and he may come to expect and make unreasonable demands on them. There is a powerful parental instinct to protect the disabled child, which may or may not be beneficial to the child. You must help him achieve a balance between dependence and independence. Encourage your child to reach out toward challenges and support him in his efforts. By conveying to him that you love and accept the person he is rather than the accomplishments he achieves, you are helping him to recognize whether failure is due to his disability or is within himself. With this insight into his limitations, he can learn to estimate his capabilities and achieve a sense of wholeness.

The handicapped child often becomes discouraged, especially if the handicap has been undiagnosed for a long time, as is often the case with learning disabilities. Discrimination against the handicapped occurs in all phases of life, at home, in school, and at work. Opportunities may be limited. It is important that parents believe in their child, that they continue trying to define the delicate line between being realistic in expectations and encouraging independence. It may be difficult to find medical support or educational assistance, but the parent must keep on trying.

Letting go, allowing your child to do more things on his own, is a sign that you have confidence in him. Expect some upsets; all children make mistakes. It takes courage to let your child learn from his mistakes. Your confidence in your child's ability is the basis for his growth in self-confidence. Let your child know his achievements give you joy, but don't wait for accomplishments to tell him that you love him for being the special person he is.

The child's physical appearance is also important to his self-image. Assist him to be well-groomed by paying appropriate attention to daily hygiene. Flattering hair styles, attractive clothing, weight control, and good posture should all be considered. "Letting go" does not mean withholding assistance when needed.

The most valuable gift a parent can give his child is a positive self-image. By guiding him, loving him, nurturing him, meeting his needs consistently and non-judgmentally, and encouraging his independence, you can provide the environment he needs to overcome emotional disability and live to his fullest potential.

The Need for Discipline

Parents must be careful not to confuse meeting the needs of the child with discipline. Emotional needs must be met, especially when the child is very young or hurting. But the time does come when you must set limits for your child. Setting limits is part of a positive approach to discipline.

Discipline is a much maligned word and its role in parenting is often misunderstood. James Hymes offers this definition: "Discipline sums up our broad goals for the child as a member of society." A noted child psychologist, Arthur Jersild, adds, "Discipline, as such, is neither good nor bad. Its value depends on its appropriateness. . . . Discipline protects the child from his own imprudence. It relieves the child of the responsibility for deciding matters over which he has no choice and thus frees his energies for action where he does have a choice. Discipline provides the child with a foundation for healthy self-discipline."

Many people think of discipline as teaching the rules of the game. The handicapped child needs discipline, just as any child benefits when parents set limits. Some allowances may be made due to the nature of his handicap, but as much as possible, treat him as you would any of your children. Common sense is an excellent guide.

Parents of the handicapped child may find that he exhibits a typical behavior. He may have learned that he can get attention with demanding behavior, lack of performance, or an appearance of helplessness. Behavior can be reinforced or diminished by the parents' reaction. By controlling your response, you can avoid rewarding undesirable behavior with attention. Many times ignoring an action is sufficient to prevent its repetition.

Occasionally some action is needed. It can be helpful to consult general parenting books or someone who is knowledgeable about your child's disability. One mother shares this philosophy: "We all come to parenting with our share of preconceived ideas, things we learned as children or have observed or read. As we put these ideas into practice, we find some that work and others that are best discarded." By combining your knowledge about your child's handicap with general parenting techniques and common sense, you can develop effective parenting procedures.

Do your best to be consistent with rules. When your handicapped child has the same restrictions and privileges as his siblings, he can more easily separate right from wrong. It may be helpful to use the same words in instructing each child. Rules should be kept simple, short, and clear.

Keep in mind that while you want to be fair in dealing with your children, each is different in many ways. Every child needs to know his parents will meet his unique needs. That doesn't mean parents love one child more than another. Jo Harmon-Blaugrund explains, "I feel a different closeness with my sick child than with my healthy one. You become closer when you face losing a child. My other son will always be special in a different way—he's my firstborn."

In disciplining the handicapped child (or any child), there are three common errors parents can make. First, they may fail to keep in mind the child's mental age and other influencing factors such as illness, hunger, fatigue, and discomfort. Second, they may not recognize the child's need for self-expression, within acceptable limits. Third, in their joy over the acquisition of a new skill, they may overlook how he is using the skill. It is natural to be so thrilled when your

Dear Erika,
When are you going to learn to copy things?
Did you know that you are cute?
I don't want you to grow up.
Because you are so cute,
And you make so many cute faces,
And I wonder when you are going to grow up.
                    Love,
                        Kathrene

Erica Wills at age five and a letter from her sister.

child has achieved a skill for which you have been working and waiting, that you neglect to check its appropriateness.

When it is necessary to correct a child's behavior, try substituting something positive for the undesirable activity. Suggest "do this" instead of "don't do that." Offer alternatives, for example, "You may not play in the street, but you may play on the patio or in the yard." A mother offers this suggestion, "When you want a child to stop doing something, give him a warning, and if possible, allow him a few minutes to stop. Use friendly firmness. Threats don't mean much to a child with a limited attention span." If the child ignores the warning, remove him from the situation.

Dealing with Sibling Rivalry

Sibling rivalry is a problem in most families, and is usually considered a normal part of family life. Sibling rivalry can actually be helpful to the handicapped child. Guard against your natural feeling of protectiveness and allow the children to work out their own problems. Handling competition and learning to negotiate are important lessons for every child.

Since the handicapped child may receive more attention and care than the other children, it is natural that his siblings will compete for their parents' attention. Explain the disability to brothers and sisters in terms they can understand. Try to be as objective and honest as you can be. Don't put off telling them nor try to hide important facts from them.

Children are marvelously intuitive and know when something is troubling you. Jo Harmon-Blaugrund recalls, "When Jordan was a few months old and we had learned of his heart problems, I wrote a poem about him. My older son, who was three at the time, came upstairs and saw that I was writing, but did not know what I was writing. He said, 'Don't worry, Mommy. Jordan's not going to die.' With a reassuring pat on my shoulder, he returned downstairs."

Your attitude will greatly determine how your children accept the problem. You may be working your way through the grieving process, but you will still need to make efforts to support your children and assist them in expressing their feelings. Give children explanations which are simple and to the point. If they want more information, they will ask for it. Try to be optimistic and honest. You may want to read and learn together.

Most parents are suprised to find out that children are more accepting of problems than the parents themselves are. As time passes, you will learn that older siblings can be a tremendous help in caring for the handicapped child. A mother remembers, "Our first-grader would proudly display his new reading

Michael and Jordan Blaugrund.

skills for his handicapped brother who didn't mind the pauses and slow sentences. Another sibling would roll a ball to the baby. They were of special help when I needed to prepare dinner or complete some important task."

Sharing in the care of their handicapped sibling makes the older children feel important and useful. Studies have shown that having a handicapped child in the family can be a valuable learning experience for children.

Less Than Perfect

Betty Wagner, one of LLL's founders, summarizes, "If your family doesn't stack up to a perfect family picture, don't despair. Not many do—but don't give up. Strong families are the backbone of any society. When we work for a strong, loving family, we are working not only for now and for our own happiness, but we are setting the pattern for future generations through our children. How better can we spend our lives?"

References

Clemes, Harris and Bean, Reynold. *Self Esteem: The Key to Your Child's Well-Being.* New York: Zebra Books, 1981.

Fraiberg, Selma. How a baby learns to love. La Leche League International reprint No. 123. Franklin Park, IL, 1971.

Hale, Glorya. *Sourcebook for the Disabled.* New York: Paddington Press, 1979.

Hymes, James. Loving guidance. La Leche League International publication No. 127. Franklin Park, IL, 1983.

Jersild, Arthur. Loving guidance, op. cit.

Wagner, Betty. Loving guidance, op. cit.

Chapter 6

Learning at Home: the Preschool Years

Many of the principles discussed in this chapter are general and may not be applicable to your child's individual needs or disability. But keep in mind that the handicapped child is a child with many of the same needs as any child. His education, though approached differently, has the same goal—to prepare him for adult living in the most independent setting he can achieve.

With all children, except those requiring institutionalization, education begins in the home, within the framework of the mother-child relationship. As Maria Montessori wrote:

> In almost all countries, the baby accompanies his mother wherever she goes. Mother and child are inseparable. All the while they are out together, mother talks and baby listens. Even if the mother herself does not speak to the child, the mere fact of

being with her brings him into contact with the world; he sees and hears folk in the street and in the marketplace, carts, animals, and other sights take a place in his mind, even if he does not know their names.

The handicapped child has a special need for the parental bridge to the world. Kathy Baker, mother of a blind child, shares her experience: "I carried Nicholas almost constantly in a baby carrier and he seemed to be very advanced in his abilities, by the standards set for most children who are blind from birth. I feel it is because of all this carrying and contact."

Charles Wills, a psychologist and father of a Down Syndrome child, adds, "The retarded child has very limited perceptions and sensations all through life. But for the first year or so the basic sensations are received through the oral cavity and visual channel." He goes on to suggest that breastfeeding is an excellent way to stimulate the handicapped child.

Breastfeeding ensures a close relationship with the mother, such as Maria Montessori described. Mother and baby are together out of necessity to meet the baby's nutritional needs, but the arrangement is also important to the child's socialization and intellectual development. This closeness benefits the parents as well. Charles Wills explains:

> It is easy to accept a normal, healthy infant, but it is much more difficult to accept a handicapped youngster during those first minutes and hours. A nursing mother somehow puts her husband at ease as she cuddles his child to her breast. The peace and tranquility exhibited by that relationship seems to rise above all the problems that may exist and the basic fact of life seems to rise up in relief—love. Retarded children can experience this in one of its purest forms—the breastfeeding relationship.

Learning at Home: the Preschool Years 71

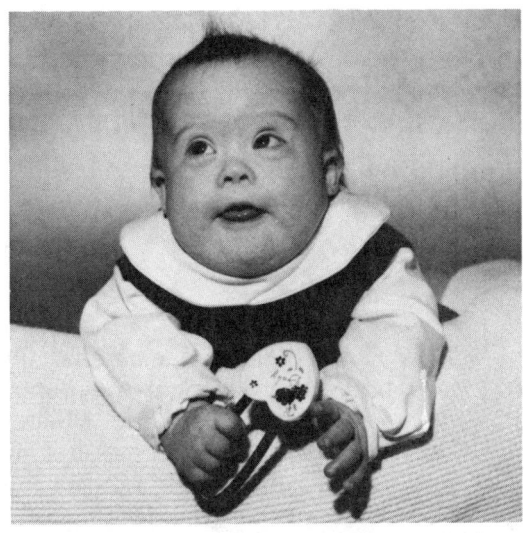

Erica Wills at six months.

Parents of these children can put aside their cares and worries for a time. They can rest assured that the nursing relationship is the first and most vital one for the retarded child. What it does for the normal infant it does threefold for the mentally handicapped child. Parents will have lots of time and practical assistance to help their special child in the years to come. But, in the first years, when they feel lonely and helpless, they can be comforted by the fact that they are doing the most for their child by nursing him.

Infant Stimulation Programs

Not everyone has this keen appreciation of the mother-infant dyad. There is a growing movement toward the use of infant stimulation and education classes. While many of these programs benefit the child by providing physical and intellectual stimulation, many routinely interrupt the vital mother-child relationship. Psychologist Niles Newton explains the importance of this relationship, "Separation from parents—especially the mother—during the first three years has a special impact on the child, because his ability to love and trust others depends on what he is experiencing in this intensely dependent love relationship."

Louise Wills shares her feelings about infant stimulation programs.

> It's not that they are harmful, but I think what is offered is better done between mother and child than in a classroom setting. What the programs seem to be is interaction—stroking, exercising, playing—the sort of thing mothers automatically do with babies at changing, feeding, or bathing times. Of course, many mothers do need to be assured that babies, even handicapped ones, won't break and will benefit from lots of stimulation. What worries me is the feeling that emanates from these programs that the baby needs outside-the-family intervention very early, that if the baby isn't attending 'school' by six months of age or less, he won't learn to sit, walk, talk, etc. Of course, encouragement never hurts, but I think it's usually best accomplished within the family setting.

An infant stimulation program which encourages the participation of the mother benefits both the baby and mother for several reasons. Teaching the mother to perform the exercises enables her to do them at home, which can greatly increase the number of times the exercises are done and the amount of stimulation. The therapist or instructor can devote more time to assisting mothers and supervising, rather than working with each child individually. When the mother is instructed in how to do the exercises, her self-confidence is bolstered. She feels better about her ability to help her child.

Preservation of the parent-child relationship conveys respect for the parents as the most knowledgeable and responsible persons in the child's life. Ignoring this fact not only erodes a parent's confidence but can also be upsetting to the parent. Kathy Baker shares this experience.

> When Nicholas turned the magic one year of age, they immediately expected me to leave him for an hour or so each week. I had all kinds of pressure put on me to leave him and go to a parent meeting alone. Even though I made my position clear—Nicholas would stay with me—one of the teachers picked him up while I was filling out some forms. When I turned around Nicholas was gone from the room. I had to hunt through two or three classrooms to find him. I was angry at this tactic which was used hoping I would just go along and not make any waves. I was called overprotective because I still maintained that I wanted him to remain with me.
>
> I explained my feelings on mother/baby separation and that I had waited to leave my older child until I saw he was ready to leave me. . . . The teacher was shocked that I would let my child "run my life." I just took Nicholas from her and walked away. My mothering style hasn't changed just because of Nicholas' handicap.

Another mother, Cathy Angell, encountered similar resistance in a preschool. She recalls, "At the nursery school, they suggested that Brian, age three, had trouble separating from me for his weekly psychotherapy session. Their answer was to suggest more separation so that he could become used to it. I answered, 'No, no, no! You don't push babies out of the nest; you let them walk away in their own good time.'

"When Brian was four and one-half he expressed a desire to go to school. Finally the time was right. We found a special school where they loved him and he loved them. They made me feel like a good mother. Brian made progress because they never pushed, but let him grow at his own rate."

Readiness for Preschool

Some children may do well in a preschool type program at age three, while others may not be ready until six or seven. Louise Wills observes, "Erika went to preschool for the retarded after her fourth birthday. At that point, her brothers and sisters were in school all day and she seemed ready for other companionship. I worried about separation anxiety, but she jumped for joy when the school van arrived!"

Many preschool programs permit or even encourage the mother to attend with the child until he is comfortable without her. Preschools for handicapped children are available in many communities, at Developmental Centers and through Head Start programs which include handicapped children as ten to thirteen percent of their enrollment.

An ideal program will provide social interaction, physical and intellectual stimulation, parental involvement, support for parents, and access to medical professionals. In any school, the parents should be involved, helping the teacher to set realistic goals, contributing to the assessment and planning of classroom activities. Whatever the program, the importance of the role of parents as advocates for their child should be stressed.

Learning at Home

For the child under three, a home-based program is the ideal way to provide needed stimulation while maintaining the mother-child relationship. One such service has been established in Columbus, Ohio by "Mother's Friend." Staff members evaluate the child in the home and teach the mother exercises to stimulate his physical and intellectual growth. Toys and equipment are often furnished as well.

As the child grows older, a training program can be initiated to assist him to fit into society, to learn social skills, and to prepare him to function in school or public settings. Because a child learns best when he feels secure, wanted, and loved, parents are usually the best teachers.

You are in the best position to teach your child because of your everyday experiences with him. You observe him daily in many different circumstances. Be alert to readiness to learn. Louise Wills suggests, "I am a strong believer in marching to one's own drum. I think that all things will happen in their own time, and that whenever a child is ready to sit, walk, use the toilet, whatever, he will. That particular time is right for him."

Learning Can Be Fun

Make learning enjoyable. Most children enjoy playing with water; therefore, skills such as hand-washing, washing dishes, and brushing teeth can be made into games initially. Children learn through exploring their environment and using all their senses. A pan of water provides many avenues of stimulation. Place a small dishpan at the child's level on ample plastic or towels. Talk to the child so that he will associate words and sounds with actions. Utilize touch by dipping his hands in the water and commenting on its temperature. Encourage him to splash to make noises with the water, or to put his fingers in his mouth to taste the water. Place a brightly colored object in the pan and let him observe it float or sink. Encourage him to reach down to pick it up from the bottom. Add a straw for new adventures.

Children also love to pour and measure. As the child's dexterity increases, provide him with measuring cups and large spoons. From a dishpan of plain water, he can progress to using soapy water and washing various objects. In winter, you can replace the water with snow or ice and let him experiment with the coldness and texture.

Play is an important part of the child's learning and maturing process. One of the greatest challenges for the parent of a handicapped child is to provide as many normal play activities as possible. Play develops physical strength, helps the child to express emotions, find new interests, and work out relationships. It gives an opportunity to minimize the disability as the child learns to do what other children do. It can be an acceptable way to release aggressive feelings and stress. Play is the road to socialization and enables the child to learn to enjoy companionship. Children need both group play and unorganized free time.

The Younger Child

The child under one can spend time on the floor, perhaps scooting, rolling, and crawling. Even when a child is unable to move about on his own, he needs the floor experience. Gesell, a noted child development expert, describes the floor as the "athletic field" of the child. Educators have found that the child who misses this, perhaps because of confinement to a playpen, may have difficulty learning to read. His eyesight and eye-hand coordination have not developed properly. Many children with disabilities can be safely placed on the floor on a blanket or pad. Exercises and games can be

Learning at Home: the Preschool Years   77

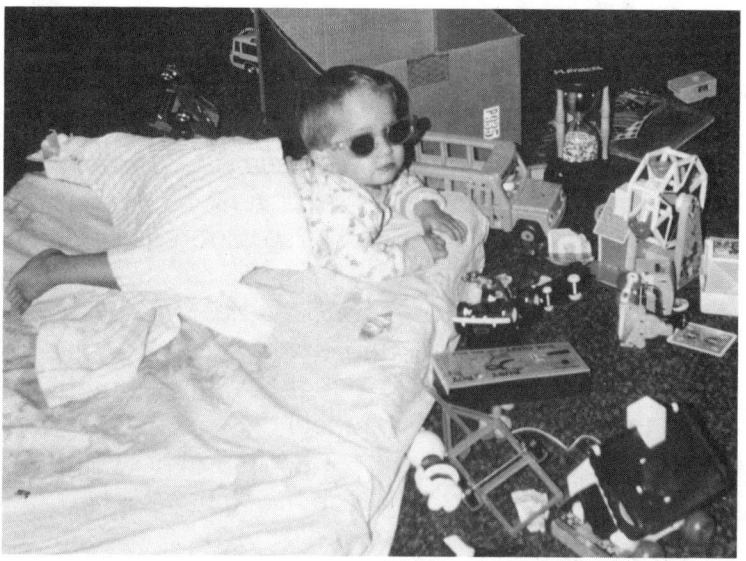

The floor can be the child's gym even when he's in a body cast.

played there. Move the child around frequently for a change of scenery and to simulate crawling or scooting. The infant enjoys motion, especially a steady rocking type. A rocking chair or a baby carrier can provide this experience.

The developmental work of the child past one year concentrates on locomotion. With the handicapped child, this may be greatly delayed but the parent can again simulate the experience by moving the child from one room to another and from one level to another. If you can devise a safe seat, you could place him in the center of a table while you do chores in the room. Certainly, transporting child, toys, and perhaps equipment from room to room is difficult, but the child will benefit greatly from the varied experiences and changes.

Enjoy the Outdoors

As a child approaches his second birthday, his expanding horizons can include outdoor play. A sandbox and swing set may be his favorites. The handicapped child enjoys outdoor play as well. Many will never have the opportunity to sit in dirt or splash in a puddle or jump into a pile of leaves. If this is the case, perhaps a child's wagon could be adapted to accommodate the child for excursions around the yard and neighborhood. Encourage him to enjoy his environment, to smell the flowers or grass, to feel the sun's warmth, to listen for birds, to feel the earth. Or spread a blanket and lie down with him to watch the clouds. Collect bits of material from the yard, colorful pebbles, leaves, sticks to take indoors to remind him of his outdoor adventures. Children of this age are great collectors and you can be thankful you have the collection in hand, instead of in his pants' pockets when washday arrives!

Music and Make-Believe

Children of all ages love music and the opportunity for motion that comes with it. A radio or cassette tapes will brighten every day, perhaps entertaining the child while you catch up on a few chores. Encourage him to draw or color while listening to the music or to dance to the rhythm.

Children of three to five enjoy make-believe. This is the perfect age for puppets and dressing-up. A ready supply of scarves, hats, old jewelry, and scraps of brightly colored fabrics provide a marvelous vehicle for the development of his imagination. Keep a mirror handy, and perhaps a camera as well to capture the

Learning at Home: the Preschool Years   79

David Good gets around outdoors on a specially adapted wagon despite a body cast.

moments of delight. Young children love to see themselves in pictures.

At about five years of age, self-expression becomes important. Children enjoy coloring, cutting, and pasting, and take great pride in their artwork. If your child is unable to manipulate the tools of creativity, crayons, clay, or scissors, you can assist him. Encourage him to point out colors, to decide where something is to be glued, to differentiate different sizes and shapes. These are all important reading-readiness skills.

Patience Is Vital

When playing and teaching, be calm and pleasant about mistakes. A show of disappointment can damage self-esteem and interfere with willingness to try again.

Show the child how to do a task, breaking it down into simple steps. One mother explained how she learned this valuable lesson, "We moved from a home with carpeted floors to one with a vinyl kitchen floor. I asked my daughter to mop the kitchen not realizing she had no idea how to accomplish the task. She threw an entire bucket of water across the floor, then tried to sponge the water back into the bucket."

Every child enjoys following adults and imitating them in daily tasks. You may need to make conscious efforts to encourage this in a handicapped child. As you work around the house, take the child with you from room to room and provide any "tools" he may need, such as a dust rag, small hand broom, and dustpan, or a piece of wood with nails and screws, a small screwdriver, and a child-sized hammer. (These should be used only with adult supervision.) Your tasks may take a little longer with your helper along but you will be rewarded watching his efforts and his pride in accomplishment.

Give help only when needed. A disabled child makes powerful demands on parental instinct to protect, which may or may not be beneficial. You can achieve balance between independence and dependence by encouraging the child to reach out toward challenges. The parent of a handicapped child needs an extra reserve of patience. One mother admits, "It's easier and faster to do things myself, but the child needs to learn to do for himself."

Learning by Doing

Chores are an excellent means of mastering the tasks of everyday living as well as providing opportunities to learn responsibility and to feel the satisfaction of accomplishment.

Begin with the preschool-aged child, with tasks which he can accomplish and which are important to him. For example, he could put a stack of folded clothing into a dresser drawer. He may need help at first, but encourage him to do as much as possible for himself. Other simple household tasks include placing soiled clothes in a hamper, watering plants, picking up newspapers, dusting tables, placing dinnerware on the table, picking up toys, putting away canned goods, and emptying a small wastebasket.

Toys provide learning opportunities as well and need not be expensive. Every child enjoys blocks. Manipulating them encourages the development of fine muscles and eye-hand coordination. Empty boxes and empty thread spools put the child's imagination to work and foster creativity. Stuffed toys of all sizes and push-pull toys are important to preschoolers. Toys can encourage problem-solving, such as fitting together the pieces of a puzzle.

Consider the durability, safety, ease of cleaning, and attractiveness of a toy. Many parents find it helpful to divide toys into several boxes and rotate them every few months so that the child is not overwhelmed by too much at one time. When interest wanes in one batch of toys, another can be brought out. You might also want to have a special collection of rainy day toys and games for those quiet times when the child is ill or hospitalized. A collection of easily portable items is ideal for car trips or doctor's office visits. These can be packed in a lunch box, ready to go. Most preschoolers love having their own lunch boxes!

Social Skills

Everyday experiences can help lead to independence. A trip to the store, library, restaurant, movie, or museum will stimulate imagination and broaden knowledge. Practice social skills which may be required on such an outing ahead of time so that you will be more relaxed and enjoy the day.

Teach the child such social skills as how to greet a person, how to shake hands, what to say, to use "please" and "thank you," appropriate ways to display affection, and so on. Practicing at home gives him experience in a secure environment. Praise him frequently and specifically to reinforce social skills.

The handicapped child needs to learn to cooperate with others, to take turns, obey rules, and fit in with others. Encourage him to develop a realistic attitude toward his disability. The child needs to be taught when and how to ask for assistance and to accept it graciously. Feeling free to ask for and accept help is part of life's normal give and take. It takes common sense to know when to task for help, to acknowledge one's limitations, and to know when failure is due to disability or to a fault within oneself. Those who cannot accept their limitations cannot feel satisfaction from their actual accomplishments.

References

Newton, Niles. They say. *LLL News* 16(Mar-Apr):22, 1974.

Keller, Julia. Program aids mothers and kids. *Columbus Dispatch*, Columbus, OH. Nov 13:11, 1983.

Chapter 7

The School-Aged Child

The school-aged child needs a variety of experiences. These might involve everyday activities such as trips to the market, library, or restaurant or those which stimulate the imagination and broaden the horizons, such as visits to a museum, zoo, or theater. There are many ongoing activities in which the handicapped child can participate. Scouting or sports programs also provide opportunities for socializing, learning skills, and enjoying successes.

Louise Wills' daughter Erika, who has Down Syndrome, plays softball, soccer, and basketball with other neighborhood children. Louise comments, "Erika enjoys movies and television. And, she spends her share of time on the phone with friends. How either understands the other is beyond me, but they have a fine time!"

Goal-setting becomes increasingly more important during the school years as the child begins mastering the skills he will need as an adult. At this time, the parents often begin to consider the future. They wonder what their child will do as an adult, what job he can hold and what social and life skills he will need. It is a natural time to seek those activities in which the disability is not a handicap, or at least is unimportant, and to find activities which can be adapted, and those which interest the child enough to encourage him to develop needed skills.

Goals and Expectations

Setting realistic goals is not always an easy task and the parents of a handicapped child may need to reassess their goals frequently. Goals arise from expectations, but parents of a handicapped child learn quickly that expectations differ from reality, as Louise Wills reminds us:

> Expectations are what we bring to our lives in the way of hopes and dreams and ideals. When our first son Timothy was born, he was the most perfect baby ever created. We knew he would be the first American pope. Today, at seventeen, he loves computers, the Yankees, driving, and being right all the time. He never mentions religion. When Kathrene arrived, she was the most perfect baby ever created. She would be a sweet and docile little girl and grow up to be a concert pianist or a ballerina. Well, for the first four months, she screamed with colic, and today, at fifteen, she is an aggressive and award-winning softball and basketball player. Daniel was our next "perfect" baby. He would become a renowned sports figure. Almost fourteen, he is active, sociable, and sensitive to the feelings of people and animals and doesn't care much for sports.
> When Erika arrived, she was the most perfect baby ever created, except for one flaw. She was one of the two in one thousand babies affected by Down Syndrome. But, we decided, she would be the Helen

The School-Aged Child

Erica Wills, age eleven, enjoys playing on a girls' softball team.

Keller of the mentally retarded, running, speaking, writing, and reading at surprising rates. Erika never read our list of expectations. Like her brothers and sister, she marched to her own drummer. She waited three years to walk, nearly six years to speak, and ten years to read. At twelve, she is, to quote her, "a big girl now."

I think if we can learn to laugh a bit at our great expectations and whittle them down to size, our lives and our children are in no great danger. The difficulty comes when we set our sights unrealistically high and refuse to recognize realities. Life would be very dull without dreams and goals; we would succumb to boredom, to complacency, to mediocrity.

Always keeping expectations ahead of us helps to minimize the otherwise deadening effects a handicap might have. Children will usually do or be what is expected of them if the expectations are within reason.

Another mother explains her goals for her handicapped son, "I want to help him develop to his greatest potential, to guide him, nurture him, help him become more secure, happy, and loving so that he will someday be able to step out into the world with confidence in his own abilities.

"As our son grew older we added the goal of teaching him self-discipline, encouraging him to be friendly and outgoing, and to develop a keen sense of humor so that others will enjoy him as much as we do."

Of course, your goals will vary depending on the nature of your child's handicap. Most parents encourage their children to strive toward the greatest degree of independence the handicap allows. Goals may be long range, such as mastering life skills, or short term, involving everyday activities. For example, one of Doris Valenti's recent goals for her son Jonathan was that he learn to walk. Because she is confident that this goal is realistic, she works with him daily to strengthen his leg muscles and to improve balance. When he does begin to walk, she will reset her expectations and begin working on their next goal.

One mother's goals go beyond those she and her husband expect of their son. "One of my goals is to maintain and nurture my marriage. I keep my relationship with my husband foremost in my life so that our marriage will continue many years after our son is grown and on his own. I also want to maintain my own personhood. So, I pursue my own hobbies and I teach my children to be independent and provide for their own needs as much as possible."

Learning and Growing

Flexibility is vital to all parents. You never stop learning and growing and should not fear change, especially within yourselves. As Louise Wills explained, couples begin their families with preconceived ideas. Parenting patterns are learned from childhood experiences, from reading, and from observing other parents. Some ideas work and others do not, and each child is different, so that parents must tailor their approach to each child's needs and personality. It is important that parents take the time to discuss their goals so that they can work together on them.

Each step forward in the child's striving for independence brings a bittersweet triumph. While parents rejoice in the child's learning and growing, there is also a pang of sorrow realizing that he is growing away from them. With a handicapped child, there may be as many steps backward as forward at times, but eventually, most children will be ready to try their wings and leave the nest.

Setbacks also occur with stress and trauma such as hospitalization. One parent explains, "With each new fracture, our son always regressed, both physically and psychologically. He became more dependent on me and exhibited the behavior of a much younger child. He required more loving support and encouragement than at other times. To say that this required flexibility is the understatement of the year!"

Let your child be your guide. If he is experiencing some trauma or stress, let him retreat into more childish behavior. Accept him with as much patience as you can muster in order to meet this needs. He will soon advance to a new stage. Try to avoid comparing his behavior to that of other children his age or allowing others to suggest how they think he should behave. You know your child best and only you can judge how best to meet his needs.

Louise Wills shares an anecdote about goal-setting with Erika.

One of my early goals for Erika was that she learn to read. I thought that even if she couldn't do other things, she'd have reading to experience and enjoy. No one thought that was a very realistic expectation. But, Erika loved books and being read to and pretending to read. At nine, she really did learn to read.

Now Erika loves to read—anything and everything. But, as her teacher pointed out to us at a conference, her comprehension of what she reads leaves much to be desired. I explained that one of my goals when Erika was an infant was that she would read for her own enjoyment. Many people thought this was a strange goal, especially for a child who couldn't speak more than a half a dozen intelligible words at age six. But my reasoning was that she would probably be limited in what she'd be able to do for her own pleasure—sports, attending movies, visiting friends, etc. My problem was, I prayed for the ability to read, but not for the ability to understand what she read!

Educational Opportunities

As the child enters school, the parents are joined by others in their goal-setting. They begin to work closely with teachers to assess abilities, to plan and evaluate the child's progress. Although a free public education has been the law for many years, it was not a right guaranteed by law for handicapped children until recently. The 1975 "Education for All Handicapped Children" Act provides a free public education, an Individualized Education Plan (IEP) for each child, and safeguards for the child and the parents. Handicapped children from ages three to twenty-one are covered by this law.

This new philosophy in education stresses the "least restrictive environment" which is compatible with the child's handicap. This may involve mainstreaming, in which the child is placed with normal

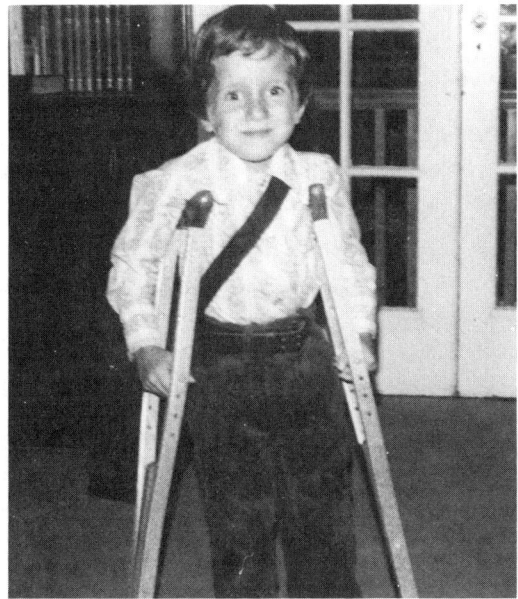
David Good goes off to school.

children for most or all of his classes. In this way, the child is exposed to the same education as the other children. It can also help the other children learn to accept disabled children.

However, there are critics of mainstreaming among educators and parents. Children with minor disabilities may prefer to be with normal classmates, but those with more obvious handicaps often feel more at ease with other handicapped children.

One mother explained that her moderately retarded child performed better in a public school than in a segregated program. She believed that the teachers in the public school expected more because they were accustomed to working with normal children of varying abilities. Her son benefited from the greater expectations his teachers had of him.

In addition, the mother points out that her son was able to establish friendships with neighborhood children because he was a part of their world. Because her son is now part of the non-handicapped world, she expects that he will assume an adult role within the community. She believes that children who are educated in segregated programs are more likely to enter sheltered adult programs and never learn to cope with the outside world.

Another mother expresses the opposite viewpoint. Her child, also retarded, was unhappy in a classroom situation where she could not keep up with other children. In a special program, she enjoyed more successes. For this child, a special program was the "least restrictive environment." This mother arranges other opportunities for her daughter to socialize with neighborhood children.

To mainstream or to segregate is a question that is addressed in the Individualized Education Plan (IEP) formulated for each handicapped child. The law provides several alternatives. The child may be placed in a regular classroom with supplemental services, such as a speech and hearing therapist. He may be enrolled in a traditional classroom but spend several periods of instruction in small groups where he receives more individualized attention. He may be educated in a center with specialized programs for handicapped children, or he may be taught at home if he is unable to attend a school.

Learn the Terminology

Just as with the medical world, parents can expect to encounter a new vocabulary in the school. The more common designations for children are:

Learning Disabled (LD)— The child shows signs of developmental learning disability rather than mental retardation. His IQ is normal or above normal, but his achievement is below the level of his IQ. He may be placed in a regular classroom with individualized attention in those areas which he needs. A "resource center" may be used for specific subjects in which the child needs special help away from the regular classroom.

Developmentally Disabled— The child may be placed in a regular academic program because his disability usually involves a physical condition.

Orthopedically Handicapped— Placement depends on the severity of the problems and the school's resources. This category includes cerebral palsy and those disabilities which can seriously impair the child's ability to work in a regular classroom. Some of these students can work within a regular curriculum but need special equipment, care, and attention.

Multiple and Severely Handicapped— The child is usually placed in a segregated program that can provide for his many special needs. The staff is more experienced with the handicapped, and the program may be geared more toward learning functional life skills. The child may have physical or mental disabilities and usually has a combination of handicaps.

Visually Impaired— The child may be placed in a regular classroom with special equipment, such as large print, or may attend a school for the blind.

Hearing Impaired— The child may be placed in a regular classroom or in a segregated program, depending on the availability of resources and his ability to cope in a hearing world.

Behavioral Disorders, also known as Emotional Disorders— The child can be placed in a regular classroom with special resources as needed or in a residential facility.

A team assessment involving a physician, school psychologist, teacher, and parents precedes placement in any program. Many factors are evaluated. Louise Wills explains the situation in her home state. "There is a Trainable Program available which is devoted less to academics and more to life skills. The usual division is by IQ—those with an IQ 50 or lower are generally placed in this program. But I think the child's motivation has to play a big part. Erika is right on the borderline, but we thought it was important to encourage her to stretch toward higher goals, so we chose to begin with the educable class. As long as she is doing well and is happy in that program, we want her to remain there. The label is not so important as the child's image of himself or his feeling of accomplishment."

As you work with the school and teacher, encourage the educators to avoid labeling your child. Categorizing a child as "slow," "retarded," "underachiever," or "low IQ" can contribute to a poor self-concept in the child and to inappropriate placement. Labels tend to produce responses and expectations which limit the child. They rarely tell the teacher if a child is capable of learning or how to go about teaching him because the child's motivation and the parental involvement and interest in education are not considered. With an emphasis on the IEP, teachers are more inclined to view each child as an individual. In cases in which there is a dispute between parents and educators over the IEP, there is a process for a hearing and opportunity to resolve differences.

Residential Schools

Residential placement is another alternative some parents choose when the child's problems are so severe that he cannot remain in the home and local school, or when the facility that can provide the help he needs is a great distance from the home. Choosing a facility is not always an easy process. The choices are frequently limited, costs involved may strain the family's finances, and the parents' emotions may be drained. A parent support group may be of help in locating a school and in providing support during this difficult time.

Parents often feel pressured to resolve the situation as soon as possible, especially when there have been long-term problems with the child in the family home. This pressure and the growing realization that the child needs help beyond what the parents and local educators can provide can trigger an emotional response similar to the grief reaction the parents felt when they first learned of the child's disability.

If you find yourself in this situation, try to remain objective and concentrate on solving immediate problems. Look at what the child has to gain from such a change. He will no longer be striving to keep up with siblings, he will be protected from an emotionally stressful situation. He can benefit from being with others who are coping with similar problems or more severe disabilities. And a good facility will encourage him to be as independent as possible.

The search for a school might begin by checking with other parents, social workers, or at the public library. There are three organizations which assist parents in locating a residential school: the National Association of Private Residential Facilities for the Mentally Retarded, the National Association of Private Schools for Exceptional Children, and Computer-Assisted Placement Service.

In evaluating facilities, check first for state accreditation and voluntary membership in the Joint Commission on Accreditation of Private Residential Facilities for the Mentally Retarded. Next consider the permanence of the facility, the distance, the cost, and whether assistance from the state or private agencies is available. In some institutions, the cost is adjusted to the parents' income. Costs may vary also between a nonprofit and a proprietary facility. Very few schools are nonprofit; most are private business enterprises. The third alternative is a state-supported school for which the cost to the parents is usually minimal. However, the facility and program may not be of the same quality as a private institution.

When you have narrowed your choices down to a few, visiting is the next step. Interview the director, discussing frankly your child's abilities and disabilities. Ask what the administrator's goals and philosophies are, what plans and aspirations he has for the future of the school. Check his administrative credentials and the credentials of the staff. Request a description of the educational and recreational programs. You may also want to know the age limit for residents of the facility, since this can affect your own long-range planning. Inquire, too, whether the school will assist in finding placement for the child when he passes their age limit. Inquire about summer programs that are available.

After the interview with the director, tour the facility. Talk with the staff, and, if possible, with other parents. Observe the children—are they playing with toys and equipment, do staff members interact with them, talking, playing, etc.? Do the children look happy? While the buildings and interiors may not be the most modern or fancy, they should be clean and brightly decorated.

Ask to see the menu for the past month. Check the kitchen and eating areas. Do staff members eat with the children? Inquire where the dishes are kept, who washes them and how. If possible observe meal preparations.

When visiting a classroom, look for teacher-student interaction. Are the children under control, what size is the class, do the children receive personalized attention as needed, what skills are stressed most? Again, the toys and equipment may show signs of wear, but they should be clean, well-maintained, and appropriate to the child's age and abilities.

In the residence areas, inquire whether the child may keep toys and stuffed animals on his bed and where he keeps his other personal belongings. Does the room have a door and is it locked at any time? In the bathrooms, are there adequate soap and toilet paper? Meet the person who is on duty at night. Check the medical facilities and staffing for everyday medical needs, and for the care and support given to the child in an emergency until parents can arrive.

Inquire about transportation and check the vehicles. Are the children properly restrained in the van, bus, or automobile? Who accompanies them on trips and where do they go? Are parents involved in school programs?

The ideal residential facility has small cottages, an adequate, well-qualified staff, a well-rounded program including occupational and social skills training, and a variety of services available to both the child and family. If possible, visit several facilities before making your decision. You will feel more comfortable with your choice if you can compare several schools before choosing the one which best meets your child's needs. Try to reach the decision rationally rather than emotionally. Placing your child in a residential facility does not mean you are abandoning him. You will still visit frequently, perhaps there can be home visits as well, and you still assume both legal and financial responsibility for him.

Whether your child is enrolled in a special program in the local school, a center nearby, or a residential facility, he deserves the best education his abilities will permit. There is a series of booklets available to parents and educators describing ways to help the handicapped child to make the best of educational opportunities. To obtain a list of these booklets, write to the American Federation of Teachers.

References

American Federation of Teachers, 11 Dupont Circle, NW, Washington, DC 20036.

Computer Placement Service, Medical Datamation, Inc. 208 Union Bank Building, Belleview, OH 44811.

Heward, William and Orlansky, Michael. *Exceptional Children.* Columbus, OH: Bell and Howell, 1980.

National Association of Private Residential Facilities for the Mentally Retarded, 1906 Association Drive, Reston, VA 22091.

National Association of Private Schools for Exceptional Children, 7700 Miller Road, Miami, FL 33155.

Practitioners' Conference on Least Restrictive Environment Placement of Handicapped Children. Columbus, Ohio: Ohio Department of Education, 1982.

Rules for the Education of Handicapped Children. Columbus, Ohio: Ohio Department of Education, 1982.

Chapter 8

The Teen Years

As Mick Ball comments, "Handicapped children have all the usual childhood problems, plus those caused by their handicap." This is particularly true of the teenage years when problems crop up for most children, whether they are handicapped or not. A mother with much experience with teens says, "Teenagers are terrific! They are fun, challenging, exciting, and noisy. Teens are a lot like toddlers; they like to venture forth and act as adults. But they also like to retreat into childhood when the going gets rough, just as the three-year-old scurries back to the safety of mom's lap."

The teen years are characterized by mood swings and mercurial changes. At times the teen doesn't recognize his or her reactions for what they are. A mother shares this anecdote, "My daughter was teased beyond endurance and had a temper tantrum, screaming, throwing things, and generally wrecking her room. When I asked her to calm down and not be so emotional, she screamed, 'Who's emotional?'"

The seemingly negative behavior characteristic of the teen is a part of growing up, similar to the negative stages the toddler experiences. In fact, in the book *Self-Esteem: A Family Affair*, Jean Illsley Clarke suggests that teens "recycle" through the same stages of development they experienced as younger children. The thirteen-year-old has the same needs as an infant for reassurance that the adults in his life will care for him and not demand that he hurry and grow up. The fourteen-year-old is similar to a two-year-old, sometimes stubborn, rebellious, negative, testing control and position. They need to know that parents do not fear their anger and that thinking new thoughts and feeling new emotions are both acceptable. The fifteen-year-old going-on-three enjoys arguing and hassling in his striving toward independence. He needs to know that his parents accept his attempts at separation. The sixteen- to nineteen-year-old continues this recycling of childish behavior as he alternately moves out into the world and returns to the safety and comfort of home.

Teens still need protection but they also need to assume responsibility for themselves. The teen years are a time for learning and growing in competence in many adult skills. The child needs to learn how to manage money, to be responsible for completion of tasks, to shop for himself, to handle daily hygiene, and to get along with others in social settings. Part of this growing-up involves emotional separation from their parents—leaving home symbolically if not physically, and returning as adults. Then, as adults, they need to reorganize the relationship to their parents.

Decision-Making Skills

The adolescent begins testing the atmosphere for separating from his parents tentatively. At the same time he is testing parental limits, he also tests himself, examining what he thinks and feels and establishing a place for himself in the family and in society. Adolescence is a time of moving from being a responder to limits set by others to becoming an initiator of one's own limits. Thus growing up involves a progression of decisions. Some of them are small and relatively insignificant, such as what to wear each day; others are more weighty, perhaps involving great pressure from peers or parents.

Parents should encourage this decision-making by first providing the framework for developing problem-solving skills. Beginning with the grade school-aged child, teach him to first state clearly what the problem is. This may require questioning on your part to clarify what the problem is. For example, when the child complains about an older sibling's accomplishment, you might ask him, "What's the problem as you see it?" His reply is likely to be, "My brother won a trophy." You might respond, "How do you feel about that?" to encourage him to recognize that the problem is not his brother's award but his own feelings of inferiority or jealousy.

After deciding what the problem is and whose problem it is, the child should consider his goal, what he wants to accomplish. Next, encourage him to stop and think before acting. Many children do not learn this step and rush into poorly conceived solutions. Encourage him to brainstorm several solutions. This teaches him that there are frequently several alternative approaches to a problem. He also learns that he can be responsible for solving his own problems because he can produce more than one solution should the first not work. Encourage him to explore the consequences of each possible solution, then try the one that seems best. This procedure for thinking through and acting on a problem may seem very involved for everyday use, but, once the child masters this approach, it will become second nature to him.

Throughout the teen years, the parents must stand back and allow the child to make his own decisions and experience the consequences. By encouraging your child to be responsible for his own decisions and actions, yet providing the support of being there when he needs you, you and your child will both weather this difficult period. Because you have provided him with the best of skills, you can feel more comfortable that his judgment and decision-making abilities are sufficient to meet demands.

Communication Skills

In addition to decision-making skills, teach your child how to communicate. Studies show that handicapped children who possess good communication skills appear happier, prouder, more creative, obedient, and more fun-loving. These are skills which must be established early in life. As one parent recommends, "If you want your teenager to talk to you, you need to begin listening when he is a young child."

Listening is one of the most important parts of communicating and one of the most neglected. The greatest compliment you can pay another person is to listen attentively. To develop your listening skills, you will need to do more than just be silent while the other person speaks. You may need to encourage your teen

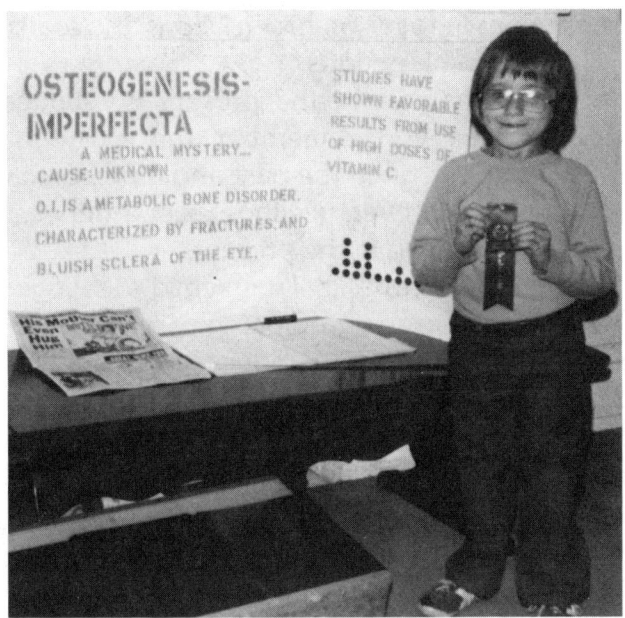

David Good proudly displays the ribbon he earned for his science project about his rare bone disorder.

to talk. There are several techniques for advancing a conversation. Paraphrase what he has said in your own words or ask if you understand his statement, perhaps saying, "Is this what you're saying?" or "Do I have this right?" You might add some self-disclosure, being careful though not to overdo the reminiscing. Relate some similar incident which happened to you. "I recall when I was sixteen, and something similar happened." The goal is to convey that you, too, were once a teen and remember the feelings and actions that are so much a part of that time, not that you want to appear superior or righteous.

Assist the teen to label his feelings correctly. State, "You feel . . ." or "You are . . ." If the feeling you suggest is not accurate, he will tell you what he is feeling.

This helps him to focus on his emotions and realize the role they play in his actions.

Bring statements to the present by suggesting, "Even now, as you remember the incident, you feel..." Events exist in the past and a person cannot change them; however, feelings exist independently and must be handled in the present.

You can be accepting of your child's feelings without necessarily agreeing by being careful not to validate the teen's perceptions. Suggest, "It seems to you that..." or "As you see it..." This is particularly helpful when the teen is baiting you into a moral or ethical discussion. It allows you to accept that he has his own opinions, which may be directly opposite your own, and to convey that he has the right to his own ideas.

Lastly, confrontation can be a useful communication tool when well-laced with empathy and listening. Point out a discrepancy between what the teen is saying and doing. For example, "You say Sue is your friend, yet I wonder why you have not included her in your activities," or "You want more freedom, but I need to know what steps you plan to take to show your readiness for greater responsibility." Return at once to empathy, paraphrasing, labeling feelings, and listening.

Communications during a time of confronting work best when you use "I" messages. Tell the teen what you feel and need. This helps to avoid being accusative. For example, you might say, "I am concerned when you are out late at night. I need to know where you are in case of an emergency," or "I become angry when I have to remove books, a jacket, purse, and remnants of an afternoon snack from the kitchen table before I can begin making supper."

Teens prefer clear, meaningful rules of conduct and limits, and want the opportunity to contribute their own suggestions in setting those limits. One mother recalls, "A fifteen-year-old foster child who was living with us continually tested our rules and limits. Finally in desperation, I gave her a pen and paper and asked her to list what she wanted from us. Just as I expected, she wrote, 'More clothes, more money, no curfew, more hugs, love, time to talk, and a stereo.' Then I told her we would work on one item at a time until we were both satisfied, and I asked her to number them according to their importance to her. To my surprise, hugs, love, and a time to talk were first on the list!"

Social Life and Sexuality

An important aspect of every teen's life is socializing. The handicapped child may be unable to participate in many of the activities of other children and, therefore, may have difficulty making friends. Mainstreaming handicapped children in regular school has helped this problem. It also helps other children get to know a handicapped person as an individual.

It is natural for the handicapped teen to wonder whether he will be able to attract a friend of the opposite sex and enjoy dating. If he has developed friendships throughout his childhood and adolescence, this will be of less concern. Peer groups are an important means through which the adolescent learns about his own sexuality.

Sex education is an area that is often neglected but is very important to the handicapped child. Sexual behavior, just like any other behavior, is learned throughout childhood. Beginning with his first questions, respond to your child honestly. This may require educating yourself first. Your family physician may recommend books or you can check the local library. If you feel uncomfortable discussing sex with your child, tell him that you are uncomfortable, but that you are willing to learn together. Children respond better to honesty than secrecy. You might also share some books with him, and discuss them together.

A child needs neither overexposure nor overprotection in education about sexuality. Listen to his cues. He is learning from peers and the media, but he needs to learn the respect for himself and others that may not be conveyed by those sources. In addition to presenting the facts about sexual intercourse and responsible behavior, you should discuss abortion, homosexuality, rape, venereal disease, and teen pregnancy.

As an adolescent he needs to know that sexual feelings are a normal part of life and that you accept his feelings. Demonstrate your respect for his sexuality by providing privacy for him. During the teen years he will be learning more about his body and its function, his emotions, and interpersonal relationships. He needs information about male/female roles and his responsibility to society to use this newly acquired information in mature ways.

The handicapped child may need additional help with his sexuality because of his sense of natural innocence and vulnerability. All children need to know whom they can trust, but they also need to be taught that there are people to fear, that some are dangerous to them. They need to learn what to do if they find themselves at risk.

You can protect your child from some types of sexual assault by teaching him about the "bathing suit" zone. This provides an easy concept for the child to understand. There are several books and organizations which assist parents and children to learn the facts about sexual abuse and its prevention.

In communicating with your teen, keep in mind that teenagers often relate better to another adult—a family friend, coach, school counselor, minister, etc. This is a normal part of growing up and it can be beneficial as long as the adult provides the type of role model the parents prefer. Once you are satisfied that this is so, you can help most by respecting this relationship and realizing that this friend is no threat to your relationship with your child.

Spending Skills

Money management skills can be taught by using an allowance system. Some parents equate allowances with chores, while others prefer to provide a minimum allowance, encouraging the child to perform extra work for additional money. One mother explains the system her family employs. "We wanted to encourage the children to handle their money responsibly and to learn about checking accounts at the same time. We give them half their allowance in cash which they may spend or save as they choose. The other half goes into an account which I manage. When they want to make a withdrawal, they write out a check for the amount they need. In this way, they can accumulate money for large purchases and learn valuable lessons about checking and savings accounts."

Second to money, a major area of disagreement between teens and parents is over clothes. One mother suggests, "We give our teenage daughter a clothing allowance and she budgets her purchases. I may make recommendations, but the final decision is up to her. If she wants to spend an outrageous sum on one item and forgo buying several others, that is her decision. She knows that when her money is gone, she has to wait for her next allowance or earn more. We've been lucky so far that most of her purchases have been sensible. I wouldn't wear them, but then, she wouldn't be happy in my choices either."

Attendance to daily hygiene is also an important skill for the handicapped child to learn. Personal hygiene and grooming enable the child to feel better about himself and be more acceptable socially. Dr. John Kriz, a dentist, points out the role of dental care as a health and hygiene issue. "Poor oral hygiene and dental problems can hamper the handicapped person's struggle for social acceptance, have an impact on other health problems, be related to the disability, and cause needless suffering."

Achieving Independence

The ultimate goal of the upheaval of the teen years is emotional and physical independence from the parents. For the parents, this means "letting go," which has been described by some as a second weaning. John Weida, Director of the Drug and Alcohol Abuse Program for Montana, suggests a plan to ease the separation, "Don't put all your eggs in one basket." In other words, don't let your handicapped child be your only interest. Spend some time on yourself and your spouse. Then when the nest is empty, you won't feel abandoned.

Each skill, beginning with crawling, is a step toward independence, and away from mom and dad. Of course, some handicapped children never take these steps, but any time they are encouraged to learn a skill or to accomplish a task themselves, they work toward eventual independence from their parents. Each step forward brings bittersweet triumph . . . while you rejoice in the child's learning, you also feel the pang of separation.

It isn't easy to let go. You have to overcome the habits of many years of protecting the child from physical hazards, unkind remarks, open stares, and thoughtless questions. When the time comes for the child to leave the parents' home, you have an opportunity to reassess your life, to make new relationships and commitments, to develop new interests. One mother points out, "It can be a shaky time. I work hard at developing my own interests, and preparing myself for the time when our handicapped child, our youngest, is ready to live independently. It has been my experience with the older children that they grow up and move out, but they don't go very far away. They come back frequently for a home-cooked meal or to use the washer. When grandchildren began arriving, I suddenly developed a new credibility and value. Each stage of our lives holds new joys and challenges. It's up to us to find them and to meet them."

With increased awareness of the role of the handicapped person in our society, there has been a proliferation of opportunities for independent living. The more severely handicapped person may choose a residential facility with twenty-four-hour supervision and total care, while the adult with less disability can live in an apartment with minimal supervision or a group home with other handicapped persons. There are special programs which combine supervised group or apartment living with employment in a sheltered workshop, enabling the handicapped person to live and work independently of his parents and enjoy the satisfaction of being a productive member of society.

Many handicapped persons marry and become parents. One mother worried that her son's disability might mean he could not father children. She discussed this with him when he was a teen and he surprised her with his accepting comment, "Well, then I'll just have to adopt children." There are many ways in which a handicapped person can overcome disability and enjoy a meaningful, full life.

Louise Wills shares her philosophy, "As we work at mothering, we need to help society recognize the dignity of the individual, the strength of the spirit, the vulnerability of the flesh and blood in the midst of technology. Natural disasters slow us down and remind us that we still don't have control over our world. Erika has taught us that there is more to life than increasing its speed. The slow-motion feeling is so true. It's amazing how slowly the picture-frames of our lives unwind, but I think I would have missed it if it hadn't been for Erika. We all need time to stop and smell the roses along the way."

References

Clark, Jean Illsley. *Self-Esteem: A Family Affair.* Minneapolis, MN: Winston Press, 1978.

Dental Care for Handicapped Persons: An Important Health Issue. National Foundation of Dentistry for the Handicapped.

Sanders, Judy. Parenting matters. *Northwest Baby* III(12):1, 1984.

Chapter 9

Handling Medical Emergencies

Every parent should be familiar with the basic steps to take in a medical emergency. Mastering first-aid skills provides the self-confidence that enables a parent to act immediately and automatically when an accident or emergency occurs. In life-threatening situations, there may not be time for planning how to act nor for waiting for trained help to arrive. Courses in cardiopulmonary resuscitation (CPR) and emergency first aid are available in most communities through the Red Cross or local hospitals, and many books have been written detailing the steps to take in an emergency.

Some general principles which apply to many emergencies are:
- Remain calm, think before acting, do not move an injured person unless his position or location puts him in jeopardy of further injury.
- Make a careful but quick examination to determine the extent of injuries.
- Check first for any breathing difficulties or obstruction of the airway.
- Next, feel for a pulse at the neck or wrist.
- Finally, check for bleeding, fractures, and other injuries.

If artificial respiration is needed, start immediately and continue until help arrives or the person begins to breathe on his own. Because shock often accompanies injuries and is in itself life-threatening, keep the victim warm and quiet until you can transport him to a hospital.

Airway Management

The first step in assessing injuries is determining whether or not the victim is breathing. Observe the chest for movement or feel the nostrils or mouth for the movement of air. Even in the absence of injury to the head or chest, respirations may be affected by a blockage and any obstruction must be removed immediately.

The tongue is the most common obstructant. Tilting the head back and pulling the lower jaw forward lifts the tongue and opens the airway. The tongue will be kept forward which prevents it from blocking the throat. If the airway is free from obstruction but the victim is not breathing, artificial respiration should be given. Follow this procedure.

1. Begin with the person lying flat on his back, head tilted back and up, airway open. Kneel next to his shoulder.
2. If the victim is a small child, place your mouth over his nose and mouth. With an older person, you can pinch the nostrils closed and cover only his mouth with your mouth. A complete seal is important.
3. Blow gently into the mouth until you see or feel the chest rise. You should be able to feel the air entering and the resistance of the victim's lungs.
4. Remove your mouth and listen for the rush of returning air.
5. Repeat about 20 times per minute for a child, 12 times per minute for an adult.
6. Continue until help arrives or the person begins breathing regularly on his own.

Control of Bleeding

Bleeding may be external or internal, and must be treated at once. Cut or tear away clothing to expose the site of the injury. Then cover the wound with the cleanest dry material available, and apply pressure over the dressing. If the site of injury is on a limb, it can be elevated to assist in bleeding control. An ice bag applied over the dressing may also help. If the wound involves the chest, a clean cloth covered by a piece of plastic is best.

Sometimes bleeding can be controlled by compressing a large blood vessel against a bone with three fingers, if the brachial, femoral, carotid, or temporal arteries can be found. Feel for a pulse in the upper arm, groin, neck, or head (next to the eye), to locate these blood vessels.

Internal bleeding may be identified by a weak, rapid pulse, thirst, and gasping or sighing respirations. The abdomen may also feel firm or rigid. If internal hemorrhage is suspected, keep the victim flat, calm, and warm. If available, an ice bag may be applied to the abdomen, and all fluids and foods taken by mouth should be avoided. The victim should be examined by a physician as soon as possible.

Cardiac Resuscitation

1. If no pulse can be found, locate the sternum (breastbone) by running the fingers along the inner edges of the ribs to the center of the chest. Place the heel of one hand, fingers up, on the lower one-third of the sternum and the other hand over the first hand. If the victim is an infant, two fingers should suffice; one hand will exert sufficient pressure for a child under ten years of age.

2. With arms straight and elbows locked, push down sharply, depressing the sternum about an inch.

3. Release pressure quickly and repeat 80–100 times per minute for a child, 60–80 times per minute for an adult. Count aloud, "One-and-two-and-three, etc.," to establish the rate. Compress smoothly and evenly, keeping away from the ribs.

4. Check the pulse occasionally to see if the heart has started on its own.

5. To combine cardiac and respiratory resuscitation, administer five to six respirations, alternating with 20–30 cardiac beats.

Fractures

If a broken bone is suspected, do not move the injured person as this could cause further damage to nerves, blood vessels, and other tissues. A skull fracture may be suspected when there is an injury to the head, accompanied by loss of consciousness, unequal pupil size, and bleeding or other drainage from the ears or nose. Avoid a pressure dressing to the head if a skull fracture may have occurred.

Fractures of the limbs should be suspected if the extremity appears to be out of alignment, swollen, or very painful. A compound fracture involves a break in the skin and the open wound should be covered by a loose clean dressing. If it is necessary to control excessive bleeding, a tourniquet may be used.

If the victim must be moved, the fracture should be immobilized first with a splint, which may be improvised from pillows, rolled magazines or newspapers, a piece of wood or board, or whatever rigid material is available. Be sure the entire limb, above and below the fracture, is supported and wrapped securely.

Never move a person with a back or neck injury. The victim with an injury to the spine must be handled with the utmost care before, during, and after immobilization of the neck and back. Only trained emergency personnel should move persons with a neck or back injury.

Convulsions

Children are more susceptible to convulsions, especially those associated with high fevers; therefore, measures to control high fevers are important. During a convulsion, the parent should protect the child from injury. He may be lowered to the floor or a bed or couch if he is in a location where he might fall or injure himself. Loosen clothing and hold the child's limbs loosely to prevent injury. The head can be turned gently to one side to facilitate drainage to prevent choking and keep the tongue from falling backward into the throat. If possible, a folded cloth may be placed between the teeth to prevent injury to the tongue, but this precaution is usually not possible once the convulsion has begun. Great care should be taken to avoid being bitten while inserting the cloth.

The parent should note the time, length of the convulsion, and any symptoms which preceded it and report these to the physician immediately. As soon as it is possible to safely move the victim, proceed to an emergency room for further treatment.

Fever

Sudden, high rises in temperature are not unusual in children and occasionally they occur without other symptoms of infection. There are two reliable methods for taking the temperature—placing the thermometer under the tongue or in the rectum. The rectal temperature reading is the most accurate.

Dr. James C. Good, a family practitioner, recommends these guidelines:

> You should call your doctor
> 1. If the infant is under four months of age and has a temperature elevation over 101 degrees rectally.
> 2. If the baby is four months to two years old and the temperature elevation is above 102 degrees rectally.

If the child is over two years of age and has a temperature of 102 degrees rectally, you may wait 24–48 hours, so long as you are treating the fever as previously recommended by your physician.

Since many handicapped children are more susceptible to infection, you may want to contact your physician sooner.

Although you can usually wait to call the physician, you should not wait to begin treating a fever. At a regular checkup, you can ask what medication and dosages your physician recommends for home use in treating simple fevers.

One of the simplest and safest ways to bring down a very high fever, over 104 degrees rectally, is a sponge bath in tepid water (100–105 degrees). The cooling effect of the water evaporating from the skin will draw off heat. Lay the undressed child on a bath towel and apply wet cloths to the body, changing them as necessary. Do this for 20–30 minutes. Avoid exposing the child to drafts while bathing. Check the temperature and repeat the bath as necessary. This should lower the body temperature a degree or more.

Choking

Choking is probably the most common emergency every parent faces. It occurs when the child inhales a foreign body or a food particle into the trachea or bronchial passageway. Coughing from the irritation follows and respiratory distress from obstruction may result. The parent must act swiftly to dislodge the object.

With an infant, place him head and face down and administer several firm slaps with the heel of your hand to the back between the shoulder blades. If that fails to dislodge the blockage, the parent can try a modified Heimlich's manuever. The American Heart Association cautions that abdominal thrusts or the Heimlich manuever **should not be used on infants or young children.**

Poisoning

Prevention is the best way to treat poisoning. **Never** leave medicine where a child might find it, even if you think he won't or can't. Be especially cautious about medicine in purses, bedside table drawers, and in other people's homes. Always turn on a light before administering any medication at night, and be sure you are awake enough to know what you are giving the child. Be sure the pharmacist labels every bottle with the drug's name and always read the label twice. If you have a question about a medication, check with the physician or pharmacist before using it. Finally, clean out the medicine cabinet frequently and discard old medications by flushing them down a toilet and rinse out the bottle before you discard it.

If the child has swallowed some medication or other toxic substance, call the physician, hospital, or Poison Control Center immediately. Read the name and spell it to the doctor or PCC personnel. Don't trust your memory or pronunciation of the medication name.

If the substance is not corrosive or oily, the safest approach for most poison ingestions is to dilute with milk or water before inducing vomiting. Vomiting may be induced by giving one tablespoon of syrup of ipecac in a cup of water. (This can be purchased at any drugstore and should be kept on hand in any home with a young child.) Or, you can give the child a drink of lukewarm water, then tickle the back of his throat with a spoon to induce vomiting.

Do not wait for him to begin vomiting, take him to the hospital or physician's office at once. Be sure to bring along the pill bottle or other ingested substance.

After the child has vomited, give more milk or water to dilute any remaining poison and to protect the stomach.

Keep in mind that the number one household poison ingested by children is aspirin, followed by other medications. Even vitamins taken in excess can be poisonous and should be given with the same care and precautions as other drugs. Never refer to medicine as "candy" and always follow the directions on the label.

Children will eat or drink anything. Cleaning fluids, paint, insect sprays, liquid soaps, and many household products come in appealing bottles which can be opened by a child. Store all products where children cannot reach them, preferably in a locked cabinet. Be aware also that poisonings can occur outside the home, at a neighbor's, grandparent's, church kitchen or nursery, anyplace where cleaning and other products might be stored.

First-Aid Supplies

Every family needs to have first-aid supplies on hand for those everyday emergencies which can be treated at home. A coffee can or other container with a plastic lid may be used as an effective and inexpensive kit which takes little space. The American Red Cross suggests that the following items be included in the kit:

1 triangular bandage
25 adhesive bandage strips
5 4" x 4" gauze pads
5 2" x 2" gauze pads
1 roll 1" bandage
1 roll 2" bandage
1 roll ½" adhesive tape
10 cotton swabs
1 small bar soap
1 small hand towel
4 large safety pins
Scissors and tweezers

If the can is stored in a car, boat, or picnic basket, appropriate coins can be taped on the inside of the lid for use in telephoning for assistance.

Permission for Emergency Care

Parents who leave their child in the care of another individual for any length of time should always leave an authorization for that person to obtain emergency medical care should it be necessary when the parents are unavailable to give their consent to treatment. By doing this, you can protect both the child and the caregiver. This form may be copied and left with the person or filed with the physician or hospital.

I, _____ (name of parent) of _____ (address) of _____ county of _____ (state), being the parent or legal guardian of _____ (name), a minor child, do hereby appoint _____ and/or _____ as my true and lawful attorney(s)-in-fact for me and in my name, for the following purposes only: To authorize any physician to provide any emergency care to said minor child, to establish a diagnosis, to administer any treatment, any vaccines or antibiotics, to administer such anesthetics and perform such operations as may be deemed necessary.

This power of attorney shall continue in force and effect until _____ (date). In witness whereof, I have set my hand this day of _____ (date). _____ (parent's signature).

_____ (signatures of two witnesses)

Child's birthdate _____
Last tetanus vaccination _____
Allergies to drugs or foods _____
Special medications, blood type, or medical information _____

Family physician _____
_____ (name, address, and home and office phone numbers)
Insurance company and policy number _____
Emergency phone numbers of family members _____

References

Good, James and Moser, Marilyn. *Guide to Better Family Health.* Columbus, OH, 1977.

Student Manual for Basic Life Support. American Heart Association:25, 1981.

Chapter 10

When a Child Is Hospitalized

Any hospitalization can be a frightening experience, especially when it involves a child. Many of a child's fears are understandable. According to the *American Journal of Nursing*, in the first twenty-four hours of hospitalization, on the average, a child will come into contact with fifty-four different people, and most will be associated with a painful or frightening procedure or unfamiliar equipment.

A child's natural fears are amplified by hospitalization. In the young child, fear of separation from parents is at its greatest. Parents are also affected by separation, as Jo Harmon-Blaugrund recalls, "I still have nightmares about being separated from my infant when he needed me most."

Many hospitals recognize the need of parents and child to be together and encourage parents to participate in his care in a Care-by-Parent Unit such as at the University of Kentucky or James Whitcomb Riley Hospital in Indianapolis. While many hospitals recognize the right and need of children and parents to be together, this policy may be limited and not apply to tests, lab procedures, or in specialized units. The Blaugrunds found that they were asked to leave during shift changes when the nurses visited each room for reports. Jo comments, "I could accept that; however, there were several times when we stood outside the door and listened to the nurses telling jokes and making after-work plans, oblivious to the fact that we were waiting to be let back into the room to be with our son."

Some institutions are beginning to permit parents to accompany their children in areas where they were previously forbidden. When Ellen Stephens' young daughter required heart surgery, Ellen stayed with Sara in x-ray, EKG, and pre-surgery until she was asleep. Ellen found that, "All I had to do was ask."

If you are able to choose the hospital, you can call in advance to inquire about the policy regarding parental care and presence during tests and procedures. If you and your child must make an emergency trip to the hospital and you are unable to make requests in advance, you may still be permitted to stay with your child, so long as you remain calm and cooperative.

Most emergency room personnel are willing to work around a parent who can demonstrate that his or her presence will make the experience easier for the child. A parent who does not interfere with the doctor or nurse and who assists in calming the child is often welcome to stay. But it is the responsibility of the parent to convey that his presence will be beneficial and not a distraction or difficulty for the medical staff.

Janice Pickett, whose son has required many surgeries, explains, "When we have been told we were

Jordan Blaugrund at sixteen months of age.

not allowed to be present for exams, x-rays, respiratory therapy, or were asked to leave the room, we politely said that we refused treatment unless we could be present. *It is important to remember that I am not talking about life-threatening situations. I am talking about normal hospital procedures.* Generally, we were told that if we thought we could stand it we could remain. Sometimes they said they would have to check with the doctor and we would tell them to do so. Stewart's doctor knows how we feel and has been very supportive."

One mother suggests, "When my son had an accident requiring suturing, I followed him right into the emergency room without giving anyone an opportunity to deny me admission. I stayed out of the way but I maintained an attitude of 'this is where I belong.' No one even questioned my presence, although I knew it was not this hospital's policy to allow parents in the emergency room."

Another mother adds, "I consider it important to give my son support when he has to have a painful procedure done, such as the application or removal of a cast. You may have to be very persuasive to convince your doctor of this. He may need to be reassured that you will be calm and helpful, that you will stay out of the way. Remember that honey attracts more flies than vinegar. Try to remain calm and reasonable when you communicate with the physician."

"Be firm and pleasant and confident that what you are saying and doing is best for your child," explains Janice Pickett.

Knowledge is one of your best assets. Educate yourself about your child's condition and possible medical complications so that you can point out symptoms to the doctor and understand better what is happening. Knowing your way around the hospital often lets you circumvent some of the routines. One mother, who is herself a nurse and whose husband is a physician, shares a story about their son's experiences. "David has had so many fractures that he is quite knowledgeable and quite authoritative about his care. When he was six years old, he broke his femur and we headed for the hospital. We bypassed the emergency room and went straight to x-ray. David proceeded to tell the technician how to place the x-ray plate and how to move him into position. As she developed the film, he said with great authority, 'Bring that x-ray over here, please, and hold it up to the light so I can see it. See, I told you it was a mid-shaft fracture. It can be cast instead of using traction.'

'We proceeded to the Cast Room and he told the orthopedic resident his diagnosis and how to cast it. David had good reason for concern because once, when we were unable to be with him, a resident cast the leg allowing the foot to drop so that it wasn't at a right angle to the leg. That resulted in a shortened heel cord which was painful for a long time. After that, David always cautioned the doctors to be sure his foot was in the right position."

Approaches Can Vary

If the hospital does not welcome your presence or forbids it, you can write a letter to the hospital administrator emphasizing how important it is for your child's psychological health not to be separated from his parents at such a traumatic time. You might also request your doctor write a note supporting your request. This then becomes part of the "doctor's orders" on the child's medical chart.

If the tactful approach is unsuccessful, you can use a legal argument. Legally, it is important for parents to be present in order to consent to tests and procedures. "Informed consent" is essential before a physician can treat any patient, and a parent who is not present cannot be expected to give informed consent. When signing the forms as you admit your child to the hospital, you could include your presence as necessary on the standardized consent form.

In addition to your presence being important to the child and necessary for legal consent, it may save your child from being the victim of an error. Many parents have shared stories of mistakes in medications, treatments, and procedures which were averted because an alert parent recognized something was not quite right. The parent is also especially sensitive to the child's individual needs. For example, one small child continued to pull the intravenous needle from his hand until his mother suggested it be put in his right hand rather than his left because he sucked his left thumb. Once his left thumb was securely in his mouth, he slept contentedly and left the needle alone.

Intensive Care

When a child is in an intensive care unit, it may be very difficult for the parents to remain with him. Janice Pickett explains, "Most ICU's encourage parents to visit but they will often try to limit the visit to 10-15 minutes three or four times per day. As a parent, you have a right to stay as long as you wish whenever you want. You do not have to abide by their time schedules. If we were asked to leave, we would ask politely, 'Is it of medical necessity that I leave?' This let the nurses and staff know that we understood their reasons but reminded them that we believed it important to remain with our child. Generally, there was no reason for us to leave."

Janice goes on to suggest:

> If you do stay and spend a great deal of time with the baby or child in ICU remember: Do not get in the way! ICU's are very busy places. Many times the staff is doing something which could mean life or death to a child. So mind your own business and your own child. Sit on a chair or stand next to the bed; do not expect to be comfortable. Most units have a rocking chair for parents, but don't monopolize it. Don't ask about other children; pay attention to your own child. Don't ask needless questions of the staff or engage in idle conversation. If you stay quietly next to your child, no one will bother you. Don't complain about the facilities. Thank the staff for whatever they make available to you. When Stewart wanted to nurse, all the privacy available was an unused treatment room with a straight chair. It was not comfortable, it was not pretty, and occasionally there were intrusions, but I was so thankful

to be able to nurse and hold my baby they could have put us in a hall or the lobby and it would not have bothered me!

Jo Harmon-Blaugrund also stayed with her son Jordan in ICU following his heart surgery. She describes her experiences. "I fell asleep in a rocking chair next to my son's crib after being up for twenty-four hours. A nurse woke me immediately and told me I was not allowed to sleep in the unit. I managed three nights without sleep, but then I just became totally disoriented." Jo's husband and grandmother were able to relieve her when she finally realized how important rest was.

Janice Pickett continues, "Ask the doctor questions about the baby's condition or discharge plans. Nurses and residents will only give you general answers, and sometimes their answers can cause unnecessary worry. Save your questions for the doctor who is responsible for your child's care." Jo Harmon-Blaugrund adds, "Always be there when the doctor makes rounds. That's when you can get updated information. Being there is proof that you are totally involved and want all information passed to you when there are changes. Ask questions, even ones you have asked before. You are under stress and memory will suffer."

Jo also suggests, "Any time anyone does something extra for you or your child, make sure you emphasize how nice it was and how attentive the person was to have done this for you. Chances are greater this will be repeated for both you and your child and for other parents and children."

Is Weaning Necessary?

Weaning a nursing baby/child who must be hospitalized is another form of separation and one which is usually unnecessary. As one wise doctor told a mother, "I wouldn't put any child through surgery and weaning at the same time."

Countless mothers have nursed babies through surgical procedures and hospitalizations. In fact, in most cases, the doctors have commented that the breastfed baby has recovered more quickly and experienced less nausea following surgery. Because breast milk is rapidly and easily digested, the baby can often be nursed within a few hours before surgery and shortly after leaving the recovery room. Even when surgery involves the mouth, such as in the case of cleft palate or lip repairs, nursing is usually the preferred method of feeding because of the many benefits, especially the immunological advantages. Dialoguing with the physician about the importance of the breastfeeding relationship to both the mother and baby usually ensures that nursing can continue. In the very rare situations where the baby cannot have anything by mouth, the mother may be able to pump her breasts to maintain her milk supply and re-establish breastfeeding in a few days, or when they return home.

Prepare the Child

Preparation for hospitalization, when possible, can alleviate many of the child's and parents' concerns. Many hospitals offer opportunities for visitation, tours, films, and special play groups for children who will be hospitalized for elective surgery or treatment. Your doctor or the hospital can provide information about this. In

Matt Valenti enjoys play therapy in the hospital after his heart surgery.

those hospitals which do not have a program, you might be able to arrange a private tour or visit for your child by contacting the nursing supervisor. Many surgical teams also make pre-operative visits to the patient to describe what he may see and do in the operating room. These are valuable services for both parents and child since many parents are unable to answer questions about the operating room. Many anesthesiologists visit before surgery to answer questions and discuss the surgery and anesthesia with the child and his parents. Your doctor can arrange this if it is not a routine service.

Lenox Hill Hospital in New York City has prepared a simple booklet for parents and children, titled, "When Your Child Is to Enter Lenox Hill." Cleveland Metropolitan General incorporates a coloring book into their pre-operative preparation. Other hospitals, New York-Cornell Medical Center, Children's Hospital in Philadelphia, and Mount Sinai Hospital in New York City also provide books for children. During pre-admission procedures, you can inquire about any literature or program your hospital offers to prepare a child for hospitalization.

There are also library books you can borrow to familiarize yourself with hospital procedures and terminology. Some, such as the Curious George series, are appropriate for children. A thorough list can be found in the U.S. Health and Human Services booklet *Books That Help Children Deal With the Hospital Experience* by Anne Altshuler.

Preparation for your child's hospitalization will include changes in your plans and schedules. Janice Pickett and her husband always tried to work their son's surgeries around vacation times from work so that both parents could be available during hospitalization. Janice adds, "When you have other children, it is hard to leave them, but we arranged the best care for them with grandparents who adored them and supported our belief that the child undergoing the most stress needs both parents the most."

Another mother says, "Sometimes in a time of crisis, there are so many demands on the parents that you don't know which way to go. You know it just isn't possible to meet everyone's needs. Setting priorities can be very helpful at such times."

Your priorities can become complicated if you have a nursing baby when an older child requires hospitalization. Some hospitals and physicians recognize your needs and those of both children and will allow you to bring the baby to the older child's room. However, many hospitals do not permit sibling visitation or children under a certain age, usually mandated by state law, in the hospital. You may be able to make arrangements for a relative or friend to stay with the nursing baby, perhaps even in the hospital lobby, where you can slip down to nurse frequently. One mother found this worked well. "When our four-year-old had to have a tonsillectomy, I took an older daughter along to play with our nursing toddler in the lobby. She was able to keep her entertained for most of the day with me coming down as often as possible to nurse the baby and relieve the sitter."

Other mothers have worked out different alternatives. One explains, "When we had a young family, most of my friends were embarked on mothering careers as well. We supported each other when a new baby came or crisis struck. We took in meals, kept each other's children, washed dirty laundry. We were family to each other."

When setting priorities, don't forget your own needs. Your hospitalized child needs a rested, healthy parent. If you are under stress, you are less likely to eat properly and regularly. If the hospitalization is following childbirth, you are especially vulnerable. Jo Harmon-Blaugrund suggests, "Try to eat whenever you have to be away from your child. It's hard to maintain any kind of appetite, but when you're nursing you need to keep up your strength."

Share your needs with your spouse and nurture each other. A small act such as bringing your spouse a cup of a favorite tea, or insisting he or she take a short walk outside the hospital will go a long way toward refreshing both of you. Some hospitals have a community house near the hospital, such as the Ronald McDonald houses, where parents can live while their child is hospitalized. Such arrangements provide more than low-cost housing; parents also benefit from the company and support of other parents in similar situations.

The Child's Fears

In addition to a fear of separation, many children are concerned about pain and injury. Discomfort is sometimes alleviated by the reassuring presence of parents. Some of the trauma can be reduced by explaining a procedure ahead of time when possible. When a lab technician enters the room, it only takes a few minutes longer for him or her to talk to the child, telling him what to expect and how long the procedure will take. The time spent in doing so will actually be less than what it might take to fight an uncooperative patient. As your child's advocate, you can request such an explanation from every person who enters the room for tests or treatments.

Always tell your child the truth. Many tests and procedures are painful and medications unpleasant. Empathize with your child, saying, "Yes, it will hurt." Give him permission to cry or say "ouch" and accept his right to hurt. At the same time, you can be reassuring that the hurt is only temporary. You might suggest techniques to alleviate fear and pain. Teach the child to breathe deeply, using the same breathing exercises that are helpful during labor and childbirth. You may also find it beneficial to use some method of distraction. Encourage the child to concentrate on pleasant thoughts or a picture. Be sure the child is prepared. Do not use distraction to allow someone to sneak up on him and administer medication or perform a test.

An older child may also fear anesthesia and losing consciousness. Some children associate anesthesia, being "put to sleep," with the death of a pet and may think they will not wake up from anesthesia. A talk with an anesthesiologist should reassure them about the effects of anesthesia.

Advances in anesthesia have made many alternatives available. Some procedures are now done under local anesthesia, with only a sedative. Modern anesthetic drugs and techniques also minimize the side effects, especially the nausea that you may recall from a childhood operation.

Children often are unable to verbalize their fears. They may not have the vocabulary, the awareness, or the security to share their feelings. They need to be reassured that having and expressing feelings is okay.

Fears are commonly expressed during play. A puppet or doll may be an excellent tool to encourage a child to work through his experiences. Some hospitals use play to assist children. Dolls might be dressed as medical personnel and patients or the child himself might be given some medical equipment or tools and encouraged to "play doctor" with dolls as patients. Such acting out can be very therapeutic.

Children feel powerless in the midst of overwhelming equipment, strange noises and smells. As one precocious toddler said, "It's my body!" Wearing his own pajamas and bringing favorite toys or a blanket from home will help. Pictures of familiar places and people and perhaps an audio cassette of home sounds, of siblings and pets, will also make a strange environment less frightening.

For the baby who has never slept in a crib, the metal cage-like hospital ones can be very upsetting. You can request a different bed, even one in which you may sleep together. However, most hospitals may object because of their fear of the child falling from a twin bed. Many mothers have circumvented this problem by climbing into the crib or junior bed, even into an oxygen tent when the child needs to be held or nursed.

Janice Pickett encountered the hospital rule that children under five must sleep in cribs when her son was hospitalized. Her husband requested a regular bed and signed a waiver assuming responsibility in order to obtain what they wanted.

She adds, "Going to the hospital is a little like going on a vacation for us when you see how we pack. We have taken Big Wheels, riding mail trucks, cowboy guns and holsters, baskets of cheese and crackers, peanut butter, and wine to the hospital. A hospital room can be a home away from home. If you are comfortable and not intimidated by hospital procedures and surroundings, your child will be comfortable."

How Parents Can Help

There are many ways in which the parent can and should be involved in the child's care. Because you are with your child you can observe his needs. For example, if there has been sudden trauma, especially one which results in a change in eating habits, you should be especially alert to his bowel habits.

The parents can be of great assistance to an overworked, busy nursing staff. You can change sheets, keep track of input and output, feed, bathe, dress the child. You can learn to change bandages, or help the nurse when she performs this and other medical procedures. Janice Pickett suggests, "Nurses are busy people. If you can save her a few minutes by making up the bed or getting the bath ready for your child, she will view you as someone who helps, not as a bother or someone who keeps her from doing her work. When you do these things, the nurses and staff tend to leave you and your child alone."

If the child is immobilized, be sure that his buttocks, spine, elbows, and heels receive attention and care to prevent sores. Keep the skin dry and clean, rubbing a little powder on pressure points. If you notice reddening or sores developing, report them to the nurse or physician immediately so that ointment can be ordered. Sores can develop quickly and are aggravated by the plastic mattress protectors and rough linens used on hospital beds. Many hospitals use lambskin or foam mattress pads for immobilized patients. You might ask for one if your child is to be bedridden for long.

If the child is in a cast, powder can be blown into it with a hair dryer, being sure to keep it away from his face. A powder with a pleasant fragrance is often welcome because after a while casts, especially body casts, begin to smell. The skin under a cast itches and the powder will be soothing.

If your child needs a medication for pain, request it. You need not worry about dependency or addiction with most of today's medications. It's a good idea to keep a record of what medications he receives and which ones are most effective. You can then offer this information to the doctor and to the admissions nurse in the case of future hospitalization.

Diet is often a problem for the hospitalized child. The food may be different or prepared in ways other than what your child prefers. Inquire about his diet and whether you can bring food from home. Many hospitals' nutritional standards are sadly lacking, and your child may be given white bread, gelatin, puddings, and carbonated beverages which are high in sugar and low in most other nutrients. The Blaugrunds did find, however, that the vending machines in the hospital carried cottage cheese, peanut butter sandwiches, and apples, in addition to candy bars. If it is permissible, you could bring in fresh fruit and vegetables, cheese and crackers, fruit juices, whole grain breads. The occasional hamburger and french fries dinner can be a real treat, relieving monotony and helping a harried mother as well.

Keep in mind your child's usual eating routine. Many children snack throughout the day and aren't prepared for a three-meal-per-day hospital regime. There may be a refrigerator you can use, and the nursing or dietary staff may be able to keep it stocked with custards, fruit juices, and nutritious snacks which can be brought out when your child is hungry. A nursing mother should also remember her own needs for frequent snacks and liquids.

Time goes very slowly in the hospital and it is easy to become disoriented. Radio and television might help as will an alarm clock or watch for the child who is old enough to tell time. With the younger child, a clock can be made from a paper plate with movable hands. If you need to leave for a short time, you can hang it near a real clock and set the arms for the time at which you will return. Even though he cannot tell time, he can compare the hands. For short times, a kitchen timer works well. It is reassuring to the child to know you will return before the timer rings or before the hands of the two clocks match.

Two other essentials for hospital stays are a flashlight and a small night light. Hospital night lights are often designed for the convenience of the staff, not the ability to get some sleep. A flashlight lets you move about the room and check the child without disturbing him. Secondarily, it is a marvelous toy—what child doesn't enjoy shining a light on walls? Be sure to have fresh batteries on hand.

Expect Some Reactions

Even with the best of experiences, hospitalization may leave an imprint on the child. Once home, you can expect some regression, a return to babyish behavior, perhaps in the form of bedwetting or thumbsucking, clinging or unusual fear of separation, anger and aggression, and nightmares. Again, play is often therapeutic. Ask the child to show you what is bothering him by using a doll or a puppet. Be patient. Children have marvelous resiliency and can overcome adversity fairly quickly.

Janice Pickett shares this thought: "Being a parent is not always easy even when your child never requires hospitalization. If you have a handicapped child or a premature baby or a sick child, remember your problems may be greater but they are not insurmountable. Love conquers a lot, and when you love your child you can be responsible for his care. You do not have to take what is handed to you. Do ask questions. Search out the experts. Secure the best care available."

References

Hormann, Elizabeth. When a child goes to the hospital. *Mothering Magazine*, 1982.

McCrary, LuAnn. The comfort of nursing. *LLL News* 19(Jan-Feb):15, 1977.

Nierenberg, Judith and Janovic, Florence. *The Hospital Experience*. Indianapolis IN: Bobbs-Merrill, 1978.

Stephens, Ellen. All I had to do was ask. *Bluegrass Babes*, *LLL News* 22(July-Aug), 1980.

Chapter 11

Communicating with Medical Professionals

Knowledge is one of the most important tools a parent has, especially the parents of a handicapped child. Learning about the disability, about medical problems associated with it, about the prognosis and treatment available, enables you to make informed decisions about your child's care and to assume responsibility for him. Doris Valenti states, "Being an informed parent is vital. You need to know what is available to you and your family and what your rights are. The more information you have, the easier decision-making and planning are."

Knowledge can also lessen concerns and fears about the future. Doris continues, "As we learned more about Down Syndrome we found it was not as devastating as we originally thought."

Learning about your child's handicap allows you to feel more in control of the situation. A person feels threatened when faced with a situation he feels inadequate to handle. On the other hand, if you feel capable of mastering the problem, no matter how difficult or new it may be, you feel challenged, not overwhelmed. The difference between threat and challenge lies in the degree of personal adequacy you feel you possess. Feeling threatened causes the individual to employ defenses which may block communication and understanding and force others into defensive stances. A challenge encourages you to seek answers and use energies in constructive ways to meet problems.

Ideally, information about your child's handicap should initially come from the physician. However, many times a doctor will only present the basic facts because of limitations of time, experience, or knowledge, or because he senses that the parents need more time to assimilate the information. He may refer you to other sources or you may seek these out yourself. The time to begin learning is immediately.

Doris Valenti and her husband recall that they were devastated by the news of their son's diagnosis, yet the very night they learned of his Down Syndrome they met with a physical therapist who works with such children. Because they had immediate answers to many questions and concerns, they found that they were better able to deal with their shock.

Information is widely available to most parents from other parents, medical professionals, support groups, and books. Even though you may not think you are ready to deal with the fact of the handicap, begin reading and talking about it. The more you learn and the sooner you learn it, the easier it will be to accept the situation and to seek other answers.

Communicating with Medical Professionals

Matt and Jonathan Valenti share a special moment.

In addition to learning about the specific handicap, you will want to investigate general subjects such as parenting, daily hygiene, education, medical care, and hospitalization. Handicapped children are hospitalized more frequently both in the course of treatment of their disability and because of complications.

Learn Their Language

It is especially helpful in learning to communicate with medical professionals to understand some of the terminology they use. As in any technical language, medicine has many abbreviations, most of which are based on the Latin words describing the body or task. For example, PO means "by mouth," from the Latin "per os."

Other standard abbreviations parents should know include:

ABR—absolute bed rest. You should inquire if this means using a bedpan or bedside commode. Some doctors believe it less strenuous to use a commode and permit its use even though the patient is on ABR.

AC or PC—before or after meals.

BID, TID, or QID—two, three, or four times per day.

CAT Scan—Computerized Axial Tomography, a computer-enhanced examination of the body which gives a more detailed picture than x-ray.

EEG—electroencephalogram, a study of the electrical conductivity of the brain.

EKG (or ECG)—electrocardiogram, a test which measures the electrical conductivity of the heart.

H & H—Hematocrit, a measurement of the volume of packed red blood cell mass by percentage and hemoglobin, a measurement of the iron content of the red blood cells.

I & O—Intake and Output, which is a record of the amount of fluids the patient receives and excretes through the kidneys and bowel activity. If the child is breastfeeding, you may have to remind the nurses to include the number of nursings.

IV—intravenous, the means by which fluids are administered directly into a vein, through a needle or catheter.

NPO—nothing by mouth.

PRN—as needed, medication or treatment may be ordered for use as needed or requested by the patient. Many times pain medication must be requested.

QD—daily.

QH—every hour. Numbers inserted between the two letters would change this to the prescribed time span, i.e. every two hours, three hours, etc.

SMA 6 or 12 or 18—blood chemistry studies of various substances.

SOB—shortness of breath.

SOP—standard operating procedure.
STAT—immediately.
UA—urinalysis, an examination of urine for the presence of proteins, sugar, white cells, other foreign cells, and specific gravity.

It is also helpful to know with whom you are dealing in a hospital. There are two types of nurses, the Registered Nurse (RN) and Licensed Practical Nurse (LPN). Both can perform many of the same functions although the RN has had more training and, in some hospitals, she is the only one who can dispense medications and perform certain treatments.

There are also differences in physicians. From the first day of medical school on, the student is called "Doctor" when he may, in fact, be a medical student. Residents have graduated from medical school and are licensed physicians who are undertaking specialized training in one area of medicine. Residents perform many procedures including surgery under the supervision of a staff physician.

Finding a Doctor

How do you know which physician you should consult? Many times this will depend on the nature of the child's handicap. The child with a neurological disorder may see a neurologist or a neurosurgeon. Both treat the same parts of the body, but the first does so in primarily non-surgical ways. This child might also need an orthopedic specialist if the medical problems involve the bones or spine. Many families find that their family practitioner or pediatrician can treat the normal medical complaints, childhood diseases, and simple accidents. For more complicated situations, the doctor may refer you to a specialist. You may want to inquire whether the specialist is "board-certified," which means he has passed an intense examination in the specialty field and maintains continuing education in that field.

When possible, make your first appointment a consultation. You can prepare ahead of time to make the best possible use of the time. State your positions as part of any discussion. In this way, the physician will see you as a valuable part of the health care team, and he will know what your preferences and beliefs are. For example, you might say, "If our child needs to be hospitalized, it is very important to us that we stay with him whenever possible. Does the hospital where you practice encourage parents to be with their children and to participate in some aspects of care?"

Discussing the Problem

If your first meeting with the physician is under less than optimal conditions, remain calm and cooperative. This may not be easy when you are feeling threatened, concerned, anxious, or perhaps even numb. Anger toward the physician is often a normal reaction because of the manner in which he presents the news of the disability or perhaps because of his reluctance to believe the parents' insistence that something is wrong. Parents often complain about the physician's lack of respect for their needs, desires, and concerns, so that hostility might be directed at the medical profession when the situation appears hopeless.

Some anger is normal and reasonable. However, it often interferes with the relationship between the parents and the physician at a time when both need open, honest, and objective communications.

Physicians and nurses often share the parents' anger. Sometimes health professionals feel threatened by a situation in which they are unable to help, to cure, or to correct. They feel anger in cases in which they cannot find or offer answers. Physicians are action-oriented people, highly motivated and accustomed to solving problems. Most of the time, they recognize and handle their frustrations because they know that they have a role in assisting the parents to come to terms with their emotions.

Don't shy away from your reasonable anger nor avoid confrontations. There is a natural tendency to avoid confrontations and to internalize anger. But when anger is clearly and openly expressed, it can help both the parents and the medical professional. Honesty is vital in developing a relationship of trust.

Throughout any discussion with your physician, remain flexible and polite, even if you do not agree with the physician's conclusions. Convey your desires and the reasons behind them, along with any reading or research you have done which backs up your beliefs. By approaching the physician in a positive way and communicating your feelings and needs, you can build rapport.

Try to remain business-like, even though it is often very difficult to be objective. Include your spouse verbally if he or she is unable to be present. When you don't understand something, ask the physician to explain it again in layman's terms. Repeat what he has said in your own words to verify your understanding.

Parental Decisions

Asking questions is a very important part of the discussion. Ask the physician for his help; ask for specific reasons why a treatment is necessary. Shift the focus to parental decision-making when appropriate, saying, for example, "You're recommending . . ." or "You're asking my consent to . . ." "I" messages are also helpful, such as, "I'm worried that . . ." or "I feel strongly about . . ." Staying on this feeling level confirms that you are the expert on parenting your child, while the physician has the medical expertise.

If the physician's advice conflicts with your preferences, beliefs, or needs, try to separate fact from opinion, and medical advice from lifestyle advice. For example, if you request to remain with your hospitalized child during a treatment and the doctor advises that your child does not need you, his suggestions are probably not based on medical concerns but on his experiences with other parents.

Hospital Personnel

While you ask a physician for advice, you are not obligated to follow it. You have the right to explore alternatives and to make informed decisions about what is best for your child.

Many of the suggestions for communicating with the physician also apply to other hospital personnel. A firm but polite attitude will gain respect while conveying your rights as parents to be involved and responsible for your child. Your role as your child's advocate is very important during hospitalization. Very often, hospital personnel do not communicate well with children. You can insist that every person who enters the child's room introduce him or herself to you and your child. You can also be certain that every procedure is explained thoroughly in a language that your child can understand, before the procedure begins.

No matter what the child's age, he should be treated with the same respect as an adult. One mother explains, "When my daughter was eighteen months old she had to be hospitalized with pneumonia. I was amazed at the nurses, lab technicians, and respiratory therapists who would come in and greet neither me nor my child. They would begin a procedure, often a painful or frightening one, without a word of explanation. By the end of the first day, my baby screamed in terror every time someone in a white uniform entered the room. Even though she may not have understood the words, a calm tone of voice and a few minutes of preparation would have eased many of her fears, yet the hospital personnel continued to treat her as if she couldn't hear or understand what was happening."

In conclusion, a parent offers these suggestions for dialoguing with medical professionals:

> Dress well. Your ideas will not receive credence if you look sloppy or are not well-groomed. Obviously, if you have made an emergency trip to the hospital you may not have had the opportunity to comb your hair or change your clothes, however, make whatever attempts you can to project an image of a person deserving respect and having credibility.
>
> Have in mind what you want to say, perhaps listed on a sheet of paper. Be well-informed about your child's needs and care, as well as general aspects of parenting.
>
> Don't let professionals intimidate you. You have the right and obligation to make decisions

about your child's care and as his parents, you are the experts. No one knows your child better than you do.

Use respect, knowledge, patience, tact, and honesty in your dealings with medical professionals.

Finally, thank the physician or nurse for his support and encouragement. The physician rarely has an opportunity to see a healthy child or a family in which all is going well. From time to time, sharing successes with him will give him a sense of satisfaction and greater respect for your role as parents and equal members of the health care team.

Chapter 12

Helping the Family Under Stress

One common thread in the experiences of many parents of handicapped children is the importance of supportive, caring persons outside the family unit. A special relationship may develop with a physician, nurse, therapist, psychologist, teacher, extended family member, friend, or another parent. As Jacie Coryell explains, "I think parents need to have someone to share with, someone who doesn't criticize, someone to watch the child to give you a few minutes to yourself, someone who will love the child no matter what."

Doris Valenti agrees, "The support of friends and family is very important. Of course, you worry about what to say. But, genuine feelings are most helpful. Tell the parents, 'I don't know what to say, but my heart is with you.' Most people feel uncomfortable when confronted with grieving parents. It may help to practice what you want to say ahead of time. Don't suggest that the problems could have been worse. To the parent, what has happened is the worst and even the smallest problems are painful to them. Avoid suggesting that they can have another child. This is the child for whom they are grieving and having another baby will not change the reality with which they are presently dealing."

Saying nothing may be better than saying the wrong thing. Jo Harmon-Blaugrund explains, "There was a day or two between the time we found out what was wrong with Jordan and the time he entered the hospital for surgery. Friends called to express their concern. One of my closest friends kept saying to me, 'I know the guilt you must be carrying.' Up to that point, I felt no guilt. We had been told there was no reason why Jordan had the defect, it was a fluke of nature. Second, she had no idea whether or not I felt guilty."

How to Offer Help

- Don't be afraid to show your own emotions. If you are a person who cries easily, expressing your emotions may actually help the grieving parent by giving him or her permission to display grief.
- Be willing to listen. It may be painful for you to listen, especially since there is a natural tendency during grieving to discuss experiences over and over. Talking about the baby or child may be the only way the parent can validate what has happened. Even though it may not be easy for you to listen, keep in mind that the parent's experiences are much more painful for him or her and you are helping by listening. Silence is often therapeutic, too. If you and the parents are comfortable

with the idea of praying together, a few minutes of silence or of prayer can be very comforting to both of you.

- Don't be afraid to touch. A hand on the shoulder, a hug, a pat on the back may actually be healing. The grieving parent feels isolated and alone. Reaching out to touch him or her will help combat this.

Write a note to convey your caring. Expressing yourself in writing may be easier and it gives the parent something tangible to read and reread. Perceptions are altered during grieving and the person is often unable to remember some events.

- Offer practical help. The grieving parent may be unable to request assistance or even suggest what you could do to help. Take it upon yourself to suggest what you might do. Taking a meal or organizing a network of friends to provide meals is very helpful. Stocking the refrigerator with nutritious snacks is greatly appreciated by parents who may be too busy or preoccupied to remember to eat regularly. Other ways you can help include running errands, performing household chores such as cleaning or laundry, caring for other children, answering the phone or mail, and shopping for groceries.

- Keep in mind the needs of the other children in the family. They may be bewildered or feel guilty. They need to be reassured that they are not responsible for what has happened. They need to be given permission to grieve, to feel sadness, loneliness, and other emotions. Encourage them to express their feelings and accept what they are experiencing even though it may not be the same as what an adult might feel.

They need to know that everything possible is being done for their sibling. If they are unable to visit a hospitalized brother or sister, photographs might reassure them that he or she is being helped. Talk to children at their own level and listen to them. When there has been a death in the family, fears of their own mortality surface. They need reassurance that they will not die and that their family life will return to normal someday. Older children may want to know what they can do to help their parents.

Children also need time away from a grieving situation. A short trip to a friend's or grandparent's house might be welcome, but any plans should be discussed with the child, especially an older one. He may feel abandoned by his parents if contact with them is limited during this time of increased vulnerability.

• Don't expect a rapid recovery. When there is a death, grief is usually limited and time heals the emotional pain. However, the grief parents experience at the birth of a handicapped child or an accident disabling a child lingers. It remains with them for life. As one grieving mother, Deborah Kiesler, explains, "Grief is a lifelong process. As we grow and mature, our loss is re-evaluated... Parents don't choose whether or not to mourn, only whether they will express grief in healthy ways."

• Maintain frequent contact with the parents. When her baby was born prematurely and stillborn, one mother wrote that her anguish was increased by well-meaning friends who thought she would not want them to visit with their babies because it might remind her of her loss. Most parents find that contact is better than isolation, even when the sight of other babies or pregnant mothers might hurt. Doris Valenti faced this in evaluating whether to continue attending La Leche League meetings after the birth of her Down Syndrome baby. She explains, "The caring and acceptance from La Leche League mothers outweighed the trauma of seeing normal babies."

- Avoid offering advice to the parents. Instead, support them in their decision-making and reinforce their confidence in their abilities as parents. The helper assists in the search for answers. Offering alternatives encourages the parents' self-sufficiency. If you offer information, be sure it is relevant to the parents' immediate needs. When under stress, people assimilate only what they need at a given moment.

Support Groups

One of the most effective methods to convey greater amounts of information and support is through a parent group. There are four basic types of groups: the discussion one in which experiences are shared, the instruction one in which most of the material is presented by the facilitator, the decision-making task force in which a problem is studied, and the discovery group, which explores problems, suggests alternatives, and supports decision-making. The last is the most therapeutic for parents of a handicapped child.

Groups differ in purpose, philosophy, goals, and the role of the leader. The parents might visit several before deciding which is most useful. For example, Louise Wills attended a meeting of a Down Syndrome parents support group, but found she preferred her local La Leche League Group. Other parents have chosen involvement in more than one group.

Groups facilitate open expression of feelings because of the capacity of the members to empathize with each other. The parents share common concerns and offer the solutions which they have found useful. In an environment of acceptance and understanding, parents can begin to accept their own feelings in new ways. In addition to receiving help, many parents find that the opportunity to offer encouragement to others is also beneficial.

Support groups are not for everyone. Exposing private family problems can be repulsive to some parents. Others are simply too emotionally and physically exhausted from caring for their child to be able to become involved. Jo Harmon-Blaugrund suggests, "Be aware that support groups may or may not function effectively for you and your child. Some groups may be heavily attended by parents who have lost children. This is a bereavement support group more than a group for parents whose children are progressing. Depending on your attitude, this may or may not be helpful."

Whether you rely on family and friends or a support group or both, keep in mind what one mother suggests, "Having family around to love your child is important. It is also vitally important to find another parent in whom you can confide, who will understand you."

References

Keisler, Deborah. Grieving is a living experience. *LLL News* 23(Nov-Dec):116, 1981.

Chapter 13

Those Who Care

With the educational and legislative changes in the past decade, there have also been improvements in attitudes toward the handicapped and in opportunities for assistance in the care of the child. Today there are many organizations and support groups for parents of handicapped children. Some of the organizations are limited to one disability while others provide more general services.

It is important that the parents of a handicapped child receive immediate information about organizations or programs of assistance. As Janice Pickett points out, "For the baby undergoing extensive hospital stays and surgeries in connection with a birth defect, financial help is available *but* this is generally available only if the proper agencies are contacted *before* the very first operation."

Along with emotional support and information, many organizations also provide practical help with appliances, special clothing, and equipment. A parent support group may not be your "cup of tea," but the other services offered can be invaluable.

The following is a partial list of organizations that may offer the kind of help you need.

General Organizations

American Coalition of Citizens with Disabilities, Inc., 1346 Connecticut Avenue, NW, Washington DC 20036 USA.

Human Resources Center, Willets Rd., Albertson NY 11507 USA.

National Association of the Physically Handicapped, 2810 Terrace Rd. SE, Washington DC 20020 USA.

National Easter Seal Society for Crippled Children and Adults (branches in every state), 2023 W. Ogden Ave., Chicago IL 60612 USA.

Developmental Disabilities Office, Department of HEW, 330 C St., Washington DC 20201 USA.

National Information Center for the Handicapped, 1201—16th St. NW, Washington DC 20036 USA.

Parents Concerned for Hospitalized Children, Inc., 176 Villa, Villa Park IL 60181 USA.

Children in Hospitals, Inc., 31 Wilshire Park, Needham MA 02192 USA.

Parents for Family-Centered Health Care, 10 Main St., Walden NY 12586 USA.

Persons Concerned for Children in Hospitals, 615 Healey Ave., Pine Beach NJ 08741 USA.

Care for Life Program, 2300 Children's Plaza, Chicago, IL 60614 USA.

Congress of Organizations of Physically Handicapped, 803 Monticello Place, Evanston IL 60201 USA.

Vantage, 2000 Center St., Suite 1110, Berkeley, CA 94704 USA.

National Association of the Physically Handicapped, 76 Elm St., London OH 43140 USA.

Parents' Campaign for Handicapped Children and Youth, Closer Look, Box 1492, Washington DC 20013 USA.

Council of World Organizations Interested in the Handicapped, 432 Park Ave., S., New York NY 10016 USA.

National Congress of Organizations of the Physically Handicapped, 1627 Deborah Ave., Rockford IL 61103 USA.

Goodwill Industries of America, 9200 Wisconsin Ave., Washington DC 20014 USA.

Indoor Sports Club for the Handicapped, 1145 Highland St., Napolean OH 43545 USA.

Intercampus Committee for Handicapped Students, 81 Electric Avenue, Somerville MA 02144 USA.

Just One Break, 373 Park Ave. S., New York NY 10016 USA.

Mainstream, 1200 15th St., NW, Washington DC 20005 USA.

National Council For Homemaker-Home Health Aide Services, 67 Irving Place, New York NY 10003 USA.

La Leche League International, Inc., 9616 Minneapolis Ave., PO Box 1209, Franklin Park IL 60131-8209 USA.

Provides information about breastfeeding, child care, and parenting in the form of information sheets, books, twenty-four-hour telephone help, and local Groups in every state and 44 countries.

Arthritis

The Arthritis Foundation, 1212 Avenue of the Americas, New York NY 10036 USA.

The Arthritis Society, Suite 420, 920 Yonge St., Toronto ON M4W 3J7 Canada.

Asthma

Allergy Foundation of America, 801 Second Avenue, New York, NY 10017 USA.

Autism

National Society for Autistic Children, 169 Tampa Ave., Albany NY 12208 USA.

National Information and Referral Service for Autistic Persons, 306 Thirty-First St., Huntington WV 25702 USA.

Birth Defects

The National Foundation/March of Dimes (many local chapters), PO Box 2000, White Plains NY 10605 USA.

Blindness

American Council of the Blind, 1211 Connecticut Ave. NW, Washington DC 20036 USA.

American Foundation for the Blind, 15 West 16th St., New York NY 10011 USA.

Instructional Materials Reference Center, c/o American Printing House for the Blind, 1839 Frankfort Ave., Louisville KY 40206 USA.

National Federation of the Blind, 1346 Connecticut Ave., NW, Suite 212, Washington DC 20036 USA.

Canadian Council of the Blind, 96 Ridout St. South, London, ON M6C 3X4 Canada.

Canadian National Institute for the Blind, 1931 Baynew Ave., Toronto ON M4Q 3E8 Canada.

Quebec Federation of the Blind, 1172 St. Matthew, Montreal QU H3H 2H5 Canada.

Bone Problems

American Brittle Bone Society, 1256 Merrill Dr., Marshalltown/Westchester PA 19380 USA.

Cerebral Palsy

United Cerebral Palsy Associations, Inc., 66 E. 34th St., New York NY 10016 USA.

Canadian Cerebral Association, 1 Yonge St., Toronto ON M5E IE8 Canada.

Cleft Lip/Palate

Cleft Parent Guild, % Crippled Children's Society, 7120 Franklin Ave., Los Angeles CA 90046 USA.

Cystic Fibrosis

National Cystic Fibrosis Research Foundation, 521 Fifth Ave., New York NY 10017 USA.

Canadian Cystic Fibrosis Foundation, 51 Eglington Ave. E Suite 401, Toronto, ON M4P 1G7 Canada.

Deafness

Alexander Graham Bell Association for the Deaf, 1537—35th Ave. NW Washington DC 20007 USA.

National Association of the Deaf, 814 Thayer Ave., Silver Springs MD 20910 USA.

Gallaudet College, 7th St and Florida Ave., Washington DC 20002 USA.

Diabetes

American Diabetes Association, Inc., 18 East 48th St., New York NY 10017 USA.

Juvenile Diabetes Foundation, 23 East 26th St., New York NY 10010 USA.

Canadian Diabetic Association, 1491 Yonge St., Toronto ON M4P 1A6 Canada.

Down Syndrome

Parents of Down Syndrome, c/o No. Virginia Association of Retarded Citizens, 105 East Annandale Rd., Suite 203, Falls Church VA 22046 USA.

National Association for Down Syndrome, PO Box 4542, Oak Park, IL 60521 USA.

Epilepsy

Epilepsy Foundation of America, 1828 L St. NW, Washington DC 20036 USA.

Canadian Epilepsy Association, 90 Eglington Ave., Suite 405, Toronto ON M4P 1A6 Canada.

Heart Problems

American Heart Association, 7320 Greenville Ave., Dallas TX 75231 USA.

Canadian Heart Foundation, 1 Michelas St., Suite 1200, Ottawa ON KIM 7B7 Canada.

Hemophilia

National Hemophilia Foundation, 25 West 39th St., New York, NY 10018 USA.

Canadian Hemophiliac Society, Chedoke Center, Patterson Building, Box 2085, Hamilton, ON L8M 3R5 Canada.

Learning Disabilities

Association for Children with Learning Disabilities, 5225 Grace St., Pittsburgh PA 15236 USA.

Mental Retardation

Mental Retardation Association of America, 211 East Third St., Suite 212, Salt Lake City UT 84111 USA.

Pilot Parents, c/o The Metro Toronto Association for the Mentally Retarded, 186 Beverly St., Toronto ON M5T 1Z2 Canada.

Multiple Sclerosis

National Multiple Sclerosis Society, 205 East 42nd St., New York NY 10010 USA.

Multiple Sclerosis Society of Canada, 130 Bloor St W., Suite 700, Toronto ON M5S 1S5 Canada.

Muscular Dystrophy

Muscular Dystrophy Association of America, Inc., 810—7th Ave., New York NY 10019 USA.

Muscular Dystrophy Association of Canada, Suite 1014, 74 Victoria St., Toronto ON M5C 2A5 Canada.

Ostomies

The United Ostomy Association, 1111 Wilshire Boulevard, Los Angeles CA 90017 USA.

Spina Bifida

Spina Bifida Association of America, 104 Festone Ave., New Castle DE 19720 USA.

Spinal Injuries

National Paraplegia Foundation, 333 N. Michigan Ave., Chicago, IL 60601 USA

Canadian Paraplegic Association, 520 Sutherland Dr., Toronto, ON M4G 3V9 Canada

A Mother's Friend

A unique project, which has served the needs of over 100 families in its first two years, is called A Mother's Friend, located in Columbus OH. Project Director Ellen Gow and her two assistants visit homes twice a week, providing infant stimulation programs, medical referrals, and support for mothers of children diagnosed as developmentally delayed. Mothers are taught exercises for the child's physical, psychological, and intellectual development. Out of the home visits, a support group for parents has grown. The program is free and has a waiting list of families who need these services. Similar programs may exist in other cities.

Other Organizations
There are other volunteer, community-based organizations which provide assistance to hospitalized or disabled children. Among these are Rotary, Elks, Lions, Kiwanis, and Shriners. Contact local branches of these organizations for information.

Government Assistance
In the fall of 1981, three-year-old Katie Beckett made the national news when it was brought to President Reagan's attention that without Medicaid assistance, her medical bills could not be paid. Yet the very system which was providing the medical care to keep Katie alive was also preventing her from being cared for at home where the expenses would have been much less. The President granted a waiver to permit Katie to go home while continuing to receive assistance. In the months which followed, other similar children were able to obtain permission to receive medical care at home under new Medicaid guidelines.

Title V legislation, which covers the State Crippled Children's programs, provides assistance for many children and their families. In addition to acting as a "third party payer" for health care, Title V plays a major role in planning, promoting, and developing medical care systems.

An example of state assistance at its best is exemplified by a consortium in the greater Chicago area involving funding agencies of the state, especially the Division of Services for Crippled Children and the Department of Public Aid. A network of services and care was developed to enable children with long-term or permanent specialized care needs to be placed in home settings.

The Illinois program involves a thorough medical plan coordinating physicians, hospitals, and other medical professionals, a nursing services plan to assist the family to provide twenty-four-hour care, financial assistance, and specialized medical equipment. The benefits of this program have been tremendous. There was an immediate cost reduction amounting to two-thirds of the expense of institutional care. In addition, the children are enjoying the benefits of a home environment and a more normal life.

Special Olympics

Sponsored by the Joseph Kennedy Foundation, the Special Olympics gives handicapped children an opportunity to participate in sports programs. They develop physical fitness and learn social skills as well. The sports events also allow the community to become involved and see the children as individuals. This exposure has helped to change many attitudes toward the retarded and handicapped.

Louise Wills shares some of her daughter Erika's experiences. "Erika has won medals and ribbons each year at the Special Olympics." This participation encouraged her to try other sports. "She plays baseball, basketball, and soccer with her siblings and neighborhood kids. Her greatest delight for the past two summers has been as a member of the local girl's softball team. She knows and understands the rules and makes up in enthusiasm what she may lack in strategy."

References

Keller, Julia. Program aids mothers and kids. *Columbus Dispatch* Columbus, OH, Nov 13:11, 1983.

Report of the Surgeon General's Workshop on Children with Handicaps and their families. U.S. Department of Health and Human Services, 1982.

Chapter 14

One Family's Experience

A local Crippled Children's Center sponsored by the Easter Seal Society may offer many activities and programs, such as physical therapy, swimming, and a preschool. Such programs often benefit the entire family as well as the handicapped child. One mother explains her son's experience:

"Because of David's brittle bones we feared letting him attend a kindergarten program where he might be accidentally knocked down and injured. The Crippled Children's Center preschool was the ideal solution.

"The teachers in the school really encouraged the children to do things for themselves and tend to their own needs as much as possible. With some of the children who had neurological disorders, it was often an agonizingly slow process. But I could see their self-confidence growing as they learned new ways to take care of themselves. I will never forget their triumph at completing a simple task such as buttoning or unbuttoning or hanging up a coat.

"I learned the valuable lesson of letting David do things for himself. It was a lot easier and faster for me to do everything for him, but he needed the opportunity to meet his own needs and the self-satisfaction of accomplishing a task.

"I saw many wonderful sights that year. I watched a little girl, who was born without arms and legs, dance. The teacher played a record and Suzie stood on her artificial legs, rocking back and forth, laughing and having so much fun that perspiration was popping out on her forehead. Another day, I held a gerbil so that she could touch it with her cheek to feel its softness. Her eyes sparkled with delight and I had to grin at my new-found courage. I don't care for little animals like mice and gerbils, and I wouldn't have held one for anyone else!

"This same child learned to swim that year. The Center Director put a life jacket on her and strapped swim fins to her pelvis. She bent at the waist and taught herself to swim. Soon she was bouncing up and down in the water by herself, laughing and having a great time.

"The Crippled Children's Center Preschool was beneficial for David in many ways. He learned that he wasn't the only one in the world with problems and he began to deal with his limitations more cheerfully. David learned to do more for himself and I learned to allow him the freedom to try, to make mistakes, and to try again.

"Getting to know the children as individuals, as unique persons, helped me overcome my squeamishness about their disabilities. When I came to grips with myself and realized how foolish I had been, I was able to enjoy the children. I wonder who learned more in preschool that year, David or me?"

Despite whatever problems you face, David Good believes you need to stop and smell the flowers as you go through life.

On Erika Weaning

The season of drought is upon us,
How sweet it has been to quench your thirst at the wellsprings of lo
You look up to the mountains now—
The valley of my breasts can no longer contain you,
I must learn to let go—
To watch you climb to your own heights,
The links in the chain of love are strong,
One wants to hold fast though nature calls to let loose,
   Fly little fledgling,
   Try your wings,
   Remember the valley of love as you soar to the mountains.

Louise H. Wills   July 19

Bibliography

Accentuate the Positive. Columbus, OH: The Public Library of Columbus and Franklin County, 1976.

Boette, Richard. Information, please. *LLL News* 16(Nov-Dec):89, 1974.

Bry, Benjamin and Benjamin, Annette. *In Case of Emergency.* New York: Doubleday, 1970.

Clarke, Jean Illsely. *Self-Esteem: A Family Affair.* Minneapolis, Minnesota: Winston Press, 1978.

Clemes, Harris and Bean, Reynold. *Self-Esteem.* New York: Kensington Publishing, 1981.

Comer, Cindy. A caring family means a lot. *LLL News* 23(Nov.-Dec):108, 1981.

Corsini, Raymond and Pointer, Genevieve. *The Practical Parent: The ABCs of Discipline.* New York: Harper and Row, 1975.

Craver, Diane. Nursing our special baby. *LLL News* 22(Nov-Dec):81, 1980.

Dental Care for Handicapped Persons: An Important Health Issue. National Foundation of Dentistry for the Handicapped.

Doman, Glenn. *What to Do about Your Brain-Injured Child*. New York: Doubleday, 1974.

Featherstone, Helen. *A Difference in the Family*. New York: Basic Books, 1980.

First Aid for Choking. American Red Cross, 1978.

Fraiberg, Selma. How a baby learns to love. La Leche League International reprint No. 123. Franklin Park, IL, 1971.

Good, James, MD and Moser, Marilyn, RN. *Guide to Better Family Health*. Columbus, OH, 1977.

Good, Judy. Breastfeeding the baby with Down Syndrome. La Leche League International publication No. 23. Franklin Park, IL, 1985.

Hale, Glorya. *Sourcebook for the Disabled*. New York: Paddington Press, 1979.

Harmon-Blaugrund, Jo. Jordan's story. *Ohio South Outreach, LLL News* 25(Mar-Apr), 1983.

Havron, Dean. Sex and depression: coping with the chronically ill child. *Sexual Medicine Today*, Nov: 14, 1981.

Hekker, Terry. *Ever Since Adam and Eve*. New York: William Morrow, 1979.

Hendin, David. *Save Your Child's Life*. New York: Dolphin Books, Doubleday, 1973.

Heward, William and Orlansky, Michael. *Exceptional Children*. Columbus, OH: Bell and Howell, 1980.

Hormann, Elizabeth. When a child goes to the hospital. *Mothering Magazine*, 1982.

Hornemann, Grace. *Basic Nursing Procedures*. Albany, NY: Delmar Publishers, 1980.

Keller, Julia. Program aids mothers and kids, and A mother's friend: a child's independence. *Columbus Dispatch,* Columbus, OH Nov 13, 1983.

Kiesler, Deborah. Grieving is a living experience. *LLL News* 23(Nov-Dec):116, 1981.

Kubler-Ross, Elisabeth. *On Death and Dying.* New York: MacMillan, 1969.

Least Restrictive Environment. Columbus, OH: Ohio Department of Education, 1982.

Lewis, Roger et al. *Child Alive.* New York: Anchor Books, Doubleday, 1983.

Linn, Dennis, and Linn, Matthew. *Healing Life's Hurts.* New York: Paulist Press, 1978.

Maslow, Arthur and Duggan, Moira. *Family Connections: Parenting Your Grown Children.* New York: Doubleday, 1982.

McCrary, LuAnn. The comfort of nursing. *LLL News* 19(Jan-Feb):15, 1977.

Miller, Mary Susan. *ChildStress.* New York: Doubleday, 1982.

Newton, Niles. They say. *LLL News* 16 (Mar-Apr):22, 1974.

Nierenberg, Judith and Janovic, Florence. *The Hospital Experience.* Indianapolis, IN: Bobbs-Merrill, 1978.

Pearlman, Laura and Scott, Kathleen Anton. *Raising the Handicapped Child.* Englewood Cliffs, NJ: Prentice Hall, 1981.

Pre-admission Orientation. Point Pleasant Hospital, West Virginia.

Reid, Gail. A dream that came true. *LLL News* 18(July-Aug):57, 1976.

Report of the Surgeon General's Workshop on Children with Handicaps and their Families. U.S. Department of Health and Human Services, 1982.

Sanders, Judy. Parenting matters. *Northwest Baby* III(12):1, 1984.

Schaeffer-Murphy, Karen. Regan's story—born with cancer. *LLL News* 22(Sept-Oct):81, 1980.

Shelling, Kathy and Dennis. Real-life drama. *LLL News* 22(July-Aug):63, 1980.

Spock, Benjamin and Lerrigo, Marion. *Caring for Your Disabled Child.* New York: MacMillan, 1965.

Stephens, Ellen. All I had to do was ask. *Bluegrass Babes, LLL News* 22(July-Aug), 1980.

Strauss, Susan. *Is It Well with the Child?* New York: Doubleday, 1975.

Thompson, Eugenie. Bonding in special circumstances. *LLL News* 20(Jan-Feb):9, 1978.

Turner, Georgia. Cleft lip. Ohio South Outreach, *LLL News* 16(Mar-Apr), 1974.

Wentworth, Elise. *Listen to Your Heart.* Boston, MA: Houghton Mifflin, 1974.

LA LECHE LEAGUE MEMBERSHIP

As you read through the pages of this book, you'll notice several references to La Leche League. La Leche League was founded in 1956 by seven women who had learned about successful breastfeeding while nursing their own babies. They wanted to share this information with other mothers. Now over 9,000 League Leaders and 3,500 League Groups carry on that legacy. League Leaders are always willing to answer questions about breastfeeding and mothering and are available by phone for help with breastfeeding problems. League Groups meet monthly in communities all over the world to share breastfeeding information and mothering experiences.

When you join LLL, you participate in an international mother-to-mother helping network, a valuable resource for parenting help and support. Your annual membership fee of $20.00 brings you six bimonthly issues of NEW BEGINNINGS, a magazine filled with stories, hints, and inspiration from other breastfeeding families. Members receive our LLLI Catalogues by mail and they are entitled to a 10% discount on purchases from LLLI's wide variety of outstanding books and publications on breastfeeding, childbirth, nutrition, and parenting.

Why should you join La Leche League? Because you care—about your own family and about mothers and babies all over the world!

Return this form to La Leche League International.
P.O. Box 1209, Franklin Park, IL 60131-8209 USA.

_____ I'd like to join La Leche League International. Enclosed is my annual membership fee of $20.

_____ In addition, I am enclosing a tax-deductible donation of $_____ to support the work of La Leche League.

_____ Please send me a copy of THE WOMANLY ART OF BREASTFEEDING, softcover, $7.95 plus $1.50 for shipping and handling. *(In California and Illinois, please add sales tax.)*

_____ Please send me La Leche League's FREE Catalogue.

_____ Please send me a FREE copy of the Directory of LLL representatives. *(Please enclose a self-addressed, stamped envelope.)*

_____

Name

_____

Address

_____

State/Province   Zip/Postal Code   Country